Strictly for Laughs

Joey Adams

Strictly for Laughs

A & W Publishers, Inc.
New York

Published by
A & W Publishers, Inc.
95 Madison Avenue
New York, New York 10016

Designed by H. Roberts Design

Library of Congress Number: 80–70372

ISBN: 0–89479–079–x

Printed in the United States of America

Foreword

This book is STRICTLY FOR LAUGHS. An onion can make people cry, but there's never been a vegetable to make people laugh. That's why I'm writing this book, to help you think funny—if you want to face a happy day.

I'll give you gags for every day of the year—and the nights too. . . . Laugh and the world laughs with you—cry and it means you can't take a joke—or even worse, you can't dish it out.

In these days of sadistic humor, you must be prepared for battle. You never know when you'll run into a heckler, a family gathering, an unfriendly audience, or a dais of opponents.

In other words, if you're looking to get laughs, I will prepare you for anything—but failure.

Would I lie to you? It is said that I am the greatest authority on humor in the world today. So what if I'm the guy who said it? Just pick out the right jokes, practice them like mad and I promise I'll make you a big comedy star—and then I'll go to work on myself.

Thinking funny is a twenty-four-hour-seven-day-a-week job and you can't strike for shorter hours. Who ever heard of a comedian who's only funny on Thursday?

That's why you have to think funny at all times, whether you feel it or not.

If you're sad, think of sad jokes: "If you want to forget your troubles, wear tight shoes." If you're ill, think of sick jokes: "I took a four-way tablet but it didn't know which way to go." Did you have a bad night? Make a joke about it. "My insomnia is so bad, I can't even sleep when it's time to get up."

Keep thinking funny. If your wife is annoying, laugh it off: "You promised to love, honor and obey—right now I'd settle for any one of them." Is she overdrawn at the bank? Don't let it bug you: "The joint checking account is a device that permits the woman to beat you to the draw." You were caught with the maid? "My wife had to let the maid go— because I wouldn't."

You look at the papers and find that your city is now putting in higher taxes, to match your state and federal taxes? Think of a funny line fast: "Help Mayor Koch stamp out take-home pay." Traffic is terrible and you may be late for your train? Grab a joke quickly: "The shortest distance between two points is always under construction."

Only your wife can louse up cornflakes? Save yourself by gagging: "The only thing my wife knows about good food is which restaurant serves it."

Don't blame the government for the tight money, just laugh at it: "They may not cure poverty, but the way they are raising taxes, they sure will cure wealth." The boss cries poverty? Laugh him out of it: "Running into debt isn't so bad—it's running into creditors that hurts."

Your wife is getting too big for her budget? Just say: "You'd make a hell of a Congressman—you're always bringing new bills in the house." Did she give you a bad day? Don't talk in your sleep—just grin.

Are the candidates too much for you? You can laugh them off the ballot: "I refuse to contribute to any one of the candidates unless he promises to lose."

For "thinking-funny" exercises, take your average day and pick out things, any things, and try to make jokes about them. That's why this is a dictionary of laughs. To give you the jokes, stories, gags, and anecdotes to exercise the laugh muscles in your brain.

Your brother-in-law drives you to the train. He's an accountant (most of them are). Tell him a joke that will keep him amused and you sharp: "You can't win when you make out your income tax. If you're wrong, you go to jail—if you're right, *you go to the poorhouse.*"

The pretty girl in your office with the lovely figure is wearing a long dress, but the ugg is wearing a skirt just below her navel. To save your sanity, think of a laugh: "The only thing a miniskirt does for her is give her cold knees."

It's very hot and the air conditioning is off. Think of a cool line: "It was so hot in Miami Beach that the women didn't carry minks—just the appraisals."

Your favorite restaurant is crowded for lunch and you have your best client with you. If the waiter gives you a hard time laugh it off: "I impressed my friends—I ordered the whole meal in French, which shook up the waiter. It was a Chinese restaurant."

It's pretty drunk out and you can't get a drink for yourself or your client. Reach out for a laugh: "Everybody was drinking so much, they had to put a sign on the menu. It said, 'Please don't tip the waiters—they can hardly stand up as it is.'"

The lunch tab is on the expense account, but even then you don't want to pay the owner's rent for the year. Grab for a joke instead of a check: "What's this five dollars for on my bill?" . . . "The chopped liver sandwich" . . . "Whose liver was it—Rockefeller's?"

You stop off at your stockbroker before you go back to the office and find the bears have eaten up the bull market. Instead of selling short or crying long, invest a joke: "Do you know what's the latest dope on Wall Street?—My son!"

You get into a taxi to go to the station and you ask the cabbie, who just sits there: "Are you engaged?" And he answers, "No, but I'm going steady." Then he wants to know where you're going because he's just pulling in or going to lunch or his tires can only go west or something. In other words, you've got to go where he wants to go. Now you get out the real laugh artillery: "You're nobody's fool—but see if you can get somebody to adopt you." Or, "If they ever put a price on your head—take it."

If he hollers: "Why should I go out of my way for you—what kind of dope do you think I am?" you tell him. "I don't know—are there other kinds?"

Now if you take the advice I have given you in this book, and pick out the jokes to match from the gag file, I personally guarantee you will be an overwhelming success as a comedian, public speaker, personality, or storyteller. And if it really works, please let me know and I'll try it myself.

Contents

Foreword *v*

The Joey Adams Joke Dictionary *1*

Institutions: Romance, Marriage, Mothers-in-law, Cheating, & Divorce *39*

Doctors, Lawyers, Dentists, & Shrinks *71*

Show Business *97*

A Dictionary of Comics *115*

Diet & Exercise *127*

Sports *139*

The Social Scene: Cocktail Parties & Drinking, Suburbia, Apartment Life, and Fashion *151*

The State of the Nation: Oil, Business, Taxes, Inflation, and Other Matters *171*

Travel *207*

Kids *217*

Age *231*

Religion *241*

Ethnic Humor *249*

New York City, etc. *259*

Strictly for Laughs

The
Joey Adams
Joke Dictionary

We're in a quickie world. There's instant coffee, frozen TV dinners, do-it-yourself yogurt, and single parents . . . If Funk and his pal Wagnall were around today, they would have to make their definitions a lot faster, sharper—and funnier.

We would all do a lot less talking if we only used words we could define, fast and to the point—and for a laugh.

Noah Webster is the fella who invented the dictionary. Actually, he was going to call it Webster's Encyclopedia—but the dictionary wasn't finished and he couldn't spell encyclopedia and there was no place to look it up . . .

Webster, the man who finally put the dictionary together, was, of course, a stickler for grammar. As the story goes, he was once caught kissing the maid in the pantry. His wife was stunned. "Why, Mr. Webster," she screamed, "I'm surprised." He answered, "No, my dear, *I'm* surprised; *you're* amazed."

I like Noah, but his dictionary needs some good gags. I couldn't give a Funk or a Wagnall for any definition that doesn't come up with a laugh.

Noah should include some of these definitions: *POLITICIAN*: A man who approaches every subject with an open mouth

. . . *DEMOCRAT*: My uncle was a great Democrat. He stole so much money he became a Republican . . . *REPUBLICAN*: The more you listen to political speeches, the more you realize why America is called the land of promise.

The Joey Adams Joke Dictionary may not make you smarter —but it will make you funnier.

A

Alcoholics Anonymous   That's where you can drink just as much but under an assumed name

Alimony   It is better to have loved and lost—providing no alimony is involved

Actor   A guy who takes a girl in his arms, looks tenderly into her eyes—and tells her how great he is

Actors   The one nice thing about actors—they don't go around talking about other people

Advice   The best time to give advice to your children is while they're still young enough to believe you know what you're talking about

Animals   If you cross a sheep with a mink, you get an animal willing to have sex that already has a fur coat

Antiques   Talking about antiques, I have an aunt who married so late in life that Medicare picked up 80% of the honeymoon

Alimony   There are two ways to escape paying alimony: stay single—or stay married

Abortion   Phyllis Diller says she was upset to hear her mother came out in favor of abortion

4

Apartments I told the manager of my building the apartment had roaches—he raised my rent for keeping pets

Appearances are deceiving The dollar bill looks exactly as it did 20 years ago

Advice Zsa Zsa says, "Fellows don't whistle at a girl's brains" . . . Her theory is that "Girls who do right—get left."

Age By the time a man is wise enough to watch his step, he's too old to go anywhere

Abstract Art Proves that things are not as bad as they are painted. Some people think abstract art is a waste of time—others think it's a waste of paint

Adolescence is the age when a girl's voice changes from no to yes

Accidents Virtually all fatal accidents happen in traffic or at home, but most people won't stay out of cars or houses

Availability Most girls find that the one quality they admire the most in a man is availability

Apartments There are three kinds of apartments in New York today: They're either going *up*, coming *down* or fully *rented*

Atheist A man who has no invisible means of support

Alcoholics Anonymous Red Skelton says he belongs to Alcoholics Anonymous, but he doesn't go to meetings: "I send in empties and get the credit."

Absentminded The absentminded guy took his car out for a walk and left his girl in the garage to be washed and lubricated

Antique   An antique is an object that has made a round trip to the attic

Advice to Loveworn   Girls, don't go looking for romance and the ideal man—a husband is easier to find

Acquaintance   Somebody we know well enough to borrow from—but not well enough to lend to

Alimony   The high cost of leaving

Apology   Only way for husband to get the last word

Ability   Is what will get you to the top if the boss has no daughter

Apartment Building   A place where the landlord and the tenant are both trying to raise the rent

Absentminded   The absentminded press agent got married and sent out press invitations to the first night

Age   Worrying about the past is like trying to make birth control pills retroactive

Advertising   Advertising can make peple live beyond their means—but so can marriage

Alarm Clock   A small device used to wake up people who have no children

Alimony   Taxation without representation

America   As the I.R.S. sees us—America is the land of untold wealth

Alimony   Like pumping gas into another man's car

American   An American is a person who yells for the government to balance the budget and borrows $10 till payday

Anniversaries are like martinis: After a few you don't bother to count them

Art Theater That's a place where the theater is clean, but the pictures are filthy

B

Bachelor A man who comes to work every morning from a different direction

Bank Where you can borrow money if you can prove you don't need it

Banker A pawnbroker with a manicure

Bargain Something you figure out a use for after you've bought it

Beauty Never marry a beautiful girl. She might leave you. If you marry an ugly girl, she might leave you too—but you won't care

Beggar "Here, my poor man, is a nickel," the lady said to the beggar warmly. "How did you let yourself get into such a sorry state?" He said, "Lady, I was too much like you are—always giving big sums to the poor."

Birthday Present What you give a wife who has everything and none of it paid for

Boss "This is just a suggestion—you don't have to follow it unless you want to keep your job."

Budget You figured your budget perfect if the money you owe is the same amount you spent

Budget Washington bureaucrats have finally figured out how to balance the budget—they're going to tilt the country

Birthday You know your birthdays are starting to pile up when people call you young-looking instead of young

Bigamy The penalty for bigamy is two mothers-in-law

Businessman He's doing very well in the business world— he had two fires and he only needed one of them

Bikini A bikini is like a barbed-wire fence. It protects the property without obstructing the view

Birth Control I know a woman who took an aspirin instead of a birth control pill. Nine months later, she had a baby who never gets headaches

Bachelor A man who has a cool head and cold feet. He leans toward a woman—but not far enough to fall

Bikinis What they reveal is suggestive—what they conceal is vital

Bigamy Bigamy is having one wife too many—monogamy is often the same thing

Bachelor A fellow who believes he is entitled to life, liberty and the happiness of pursuit

C

Cars Nowadays if you want to buy a $10,000 car it's easy— buy a $3,000 car on time!

Cheap He's the first to put his hand in his pocket—and keep it there

Chinese and Japanese How can you tell the Chinese from the Japanese? Easy! The Japanese have cars and the Chinese have bicycles—made in Japan

Chrysler Mr. Whipple, the Charmin-man, has a special on three-ply Chrysler stock certificates

Community Property Law "I realize a wife is entitled to half of everything—but *not* in *advance*."

Computers There is a computer that is so human that when it breaks down they don't give it oil—they give it coffee

Credit I tried to use my Master-Card in a health food store and the clerk told me they only accept natural cash

Credit Cards Credit cards have three dimensions: height, width, and debt

Career Girls A career girl is a woman who goes out and earns a man's salary instead of staying home and taking it away from him

Charity To enjoy a good reputation, give publicly and steal privately

Credit Cards Credit cards are what people use after they discover that money can't buy everything

Charity As the minister said, "Let's give freely and generously—as reported to the Internal Revenue Service."

Children Children are not only a comfort to a man when he reaches middle age—they help bring it on

Communist A person who has given up all hope of becoming a capitalist

Counterfeiter A counterfeiter is a man who gets into trouble by following a good example

Credit Cards A credit card is a printed I.O.U.—today you need a credit card to pay cash

Credit Card You can pay for everything these days with a credit card—except the monthly bills you run up with it

Cookbook Pat Cooper told his wife that for a new and exciting meal she should try the Galloping Gourmet's cookbook—so she boiled it

Crime in the Streets That's the price of the new cars

Communism In Russia when you call information—you better have some. At a church in Moscow the sign says, "In praying, keep your eyes closed at your own risk."

Credit For the man who has everything: A calendar to remind him when the payments are due

Chaperone An old maid who never made the first team—but she's still intercepting passes

Crime The laws are strictly for the crooks. They lock up the witness and the jury—and they let the prisoner out on bail

Confusion Anybody who isn't confused today isn't well informed

Chrysler Chrysler is having trouble getting their money because the government can't figure out if it's okay to give money to Americans

Cheap The only time he'll pick up a check is if it's made out to him

Child Training Is chiefly a matter of knowing which end to pat—and when . . . Kids rarely misquote you—especially when they repeat what you shouldn't have said

Cuba Lee Tully says he can't understand Cuba: The capital is Havana, the government is Moscow, and all the people live in Miami

Conservative A conservative goes to a nude movie for the message—or to a French picture and reads the titles

Congress Where a man gets up to speak, says nothing, nobody listens—and then everybody disagrees

Communism In Russia there is freedom of speech—but there is no guarantee of freedom *after* speech

Crime Crime doesn't pay—every murderer sooner or later gets a ticket for parking

Credit Use our easy credit plan: 100 percent down—no payments

Communist Someone who has nothing and wants to share it with everybody

D

Divorce Is when a husband no longer has to bring the money home to his wife—he can mail it

Diet It's easy to diet these days—just eat what you can afford

Doctor My doctor doesn't believe in unnecessary surgery. He won't operate unless he absolutely needs the money

Divorce Divorce has done more to promote peace than the U.N. Divorce is useless. You get married for lack of judgment, you get divorced for lack of patience—then you remarry for lack of memory

Drive-In Theater There's a new drive-in theater screen—the manager puts one around each car

Disco I don't like those wild disco dancers. I like slow dancing. When I'm dancing with a girl, I like to know what I'm up against

Doctors Ralph Nader classified doctors into three types— expensive, costly, and exorbitant

Diet Willpower is when a guy is going to the chair, has his last meal—and stays on Weight Watchers

Diet Today you can go on a steak diet and lose $200 in a week

Draft Congress is rushing through a draft law for all 19- and 20-year-olds—and Greyhound is putting on double buses, all bound for Canada

Dumb-Dumb Passing a police station, this dumb-dumb saw a notice: "Man wanted for rape"—so he went inside and applied for the job

Diet I lost 20 pounds by giving up only two things—a knife and a fork

Despair Is when you get kidnapped—and your wife tries to put the ransom on MasterCard

Diet He went on the drinking man's diet. In only three weeks he lost 21 days and his job

Diplomat A man who can convince his wife she looks vulgar in diamonds—and fat in a mink coat

Diplomacy The ability to take something and act as though you were giving it away . . . A good diplomat is one who knows what to talk about, but never talks about what he knows

Divorce The three chief causes of divorce are men, women, and marriage . . .

Disc Jockey Every time we hear a disc jockey play the top 40 tunes, we get the shakes thinking what the bottom 40 must sound like

Drive-In Just think what a drive-in would be called if there were nothing on the screen

Doctors God heals and the doctor collects the fee

Doctors Some doctors tell their patients the worst—others mail the bill

Drunk He has wonderful self-control. He never drinks unless someone else is buying

Diet The way food prices are going up, being overweight may soon be a status symbol

Diplomacy Is the art of letting someone have your way

Drive-In Theater No matter how bad the movie is at a drive-in theater, most patrons love every minute of it

Doormen A doorman is a genius who opens your taxi door with one hand, helps you in with the other, and still has a hand left waiting for the tip

Diet They say that people who are disappointed in love are compulsive eaters. So how come there are so many fat sultans?

Diplomat The perfect diplomat praises married life but remains single. When a diplomat says yes he means perhaps —when he says perhaps he means no—when he says no he is no diplomat

Doctor He's the kind of doctor that feels your purse

Diplomat A person who can be disarming—even though his country isn't

E

Err   To err is human—but isn't it divine?

Executive   A good executive is a man who wears the worried look—upon his assistant's face

Exercise   Red Skelton says, "The only exercise I get is acting as pallbearer for my friends who exercise."

Efficiency Expert   A guy smart enough to tell you how to run your business and too smart to start his own

Employment   I love my job—it's the work I hate

Egghead   A character who has found something more interesting than a woman

Egotist   A man who talks about himself—when you want to talk about *yourself*

Economists   If all the economists were laid end to end, they would not reach a conclusion . . . The secret of economy is to live as cheaply the first few days after payday as you lived the last few days before

Education   What parents get when they talk to teenagers

Education   That's something a boy spends years getting—so he can work for a man who has no education at all

Economy   We're living in a great economy—I never spent so much taxes in my life

Elections   Elections are things that are held to see if the polls were right

Electric Bill   I can't believe our electric bill. I'll just have to keep our thermostat at no more than 62—dollars per day

14

Exercise If it weren't for the fact that the TV set and the refrigerator are so far apart, some of us wouldn't get any exercise at all

Extravagant Throwing out a teabag after using it only once

F

Foreign Policy Our foreign aid is based on a strict policy of exchanging American dollars for bad will

Fashion The best thing about the latest fashion for women is that it won't last . . . It's the men who pay the bills who are the real slaves to fashion

Father and Son My neighbor says he has four sons and not one will come when he calls. They'll probably grow up to be doctors—or waiters

Fashion The only women who dress to please their husbands are wearing last year's clothes

Flying There's still a bit of risk in aviation—the taxi ride from the city to the airport

Figure My neighbor's wife has everything. The only trouble is that it all settles in one place

Fan Club A group of people who tell an actor he is not alone in the way he feels about himself

Fat His suits are being converted into condominiums

Foreign Aid Somebody suggested to Mayor Koch that new York secede from the Union and form a new country. Then we can apply for foreign aid

Frustration and Panic Frustration is the first time you discover you can't do it the second time. Panic is the second time you discover you can't do it the first time

Fat Farms I really think those fat farms are ridiculous—I mean, spending $1,000 to take off what it cost you $10,000 to put on

Fat Farms I went to one of those fat farms and they really work—the first day alone I was $500 lighter

Family Man One who has replaced the currency in his wallet with snapshots

Fair-Weather Friend One who is always around when he needs you

Fashion When a husband talks about the height of fashion —he probably means the prices

Fashion A wise man never laughs at his wife's old clothes . . . As the boutique manager explained: "But madam, looking ridiculous is the fashion this year!"

Father The kin you love to touch

G

Gossip Make someone happy—mind your own business

Gossip Most people can keep a secret. It's the ones they tell it to that can't

Gambling The only way to win at blackjack is to use a real blackjack

Gas I left my car at the gas station and asked them to fill it up. They asked for collateral

Gossip More people are run down by gossip than by automobiles . . . You can't believe everything you hear, but you can repeat it

Grandchildren One of the great mysteries of life is how the boy who wasn't good enough to marry the daughter can be the father of the smartest grandchild in the world

Gambling My friend Earl Wilson was describing the '29 crash as "A time when billions were lost and so many were ruined." Milton Berle interjected: "An average day in Las Vegas . . ." Zsa Zsa Gabor has a tip for all wives to prevent their husbands from gambling: "Spend it first."

Gambling Don't gamble unless you can afford to lose. And if you can afford to lose—you don't have to gamble

Garden A garden is a thing of beauty and a job forever

Grammar I asked my tailor to settle a problem. I wanted to know if "pants" is singular or plural. The tailor said, "Both are correct—pants are singular on top and plural on the bottom."

Gas Prices If gas prices continue to spiral an optional accessory on the 1981 cars will be a bus ticket

Government Any government that is big enough to give you everything you want is big enough to take everything you've got

Grandparent The cheapest toy, which even a young child can operate, is called a grandparent

Gigolos Hired hands

Gas Stations No gas station is totally self service—they still have somebody there to take your money

Gambling Gamblers are nice people. I have one friend who always observes "Be Kind to Animals Week." All the money he earns he gives to the horses

H

Heart When a woman's heart is in the right place, it may be a sign she isn't wearing a girdle

Health The best way to keep healthy is to eat what you don't want, drink what you don't like, and do what you'd rather not

Humanitarian He's a real humanitarian—he just opened a halfway house for girls who won't go all the way

Heredity Is what you believe in until your kid starts acting like a delinquent

Honeymoon The honeymoon is over when he gets out of the car at the drive-in movie to wipe off the windshield

Husband The average man has probably thought twice about running away from home—once as a child and once as a husband

Hollywood Is where you spend more than you make, on things you don't need—to impress people you don't like

Hotels Why are hotel room walls so thin when you sleep and so thick when you listen?

Honesty It's strange that man should take up crime when there are so many legal ways to be dishonest

Happiness   Happiness is a vegetarian looking at the price of meat today

Hospital Room   A place where friends of the patient meet to talk to other friends of the patient

Hookers   Hookers in Manhattan are wearing T-shirts that say, "I love N.Y.—one at a time."

Home   We finally found a charming little house we can afford—if we can just get it out of the tree

Hindsight   What a woman should have before wearing jeans

Health   In America we spend billions of dollars a year just for health—no wonder we have so many healthy doctors

Happiness   That's when an old man marries a frigid woman

Horror Stories   If you like a good horror story—go home and read your electric meter

Hospital   That's a place that keeps you three days if you have big troubles and three months if you have big insurance

Hospital Bed   A parked taxi with the meter running

Housewife   A housewife is someone who spends seven days a week cleaning house, shopping for food, cooking meals, washing, ironing, and being a valet, maid, and chauffeur for the kids. But that doesn't really hurt. What hurts is when somebody asks her husband, "Does your wife work?" and he says, "No."

Hospitals   There should be an intensive care unit right next to the cashier's office

Housekeeper   Zsa Zsa Gabor is a great housekeeper. Every time she gets divorced she keeps the house

I

Insurance With all of today's attractive accident policies, a man can't afford to die a natural death

Income Tax Another way of spring cleaning your bank account

Israel You've got to give Israel credit—the only thing chicken about them is their soup

I.R.S. Does it ever occur to you that your paycheck has turned into a receipt for your payroll deductions?

Inflation A little inflation is like a little pregnancy—it keeps on growing

Inflation We have the highest standard of living in the world—too bad we can't afford it . . . There's consolation in inflation: the money you haven't got isn't worth as much as it used to

Inventions Nowadays, to make a fortune you have to come out with something that is low-priced, habit-forming, and tax-deductible

Insults Joan Rivers noted, "It's hard to describe Milton Berle. It's like trying to explain a cigar butt in an old maid's bedroom . . ." Berle said, "Joan was born in show business and after her last picture, she died in it . . ."

I.R.S. The income tax guys must love poor people—they're creating so many of them

Inflation There are a lot of things money can't buy—for instance, what it did last month

Inflation If we put the post office in charge of inflation, they might not stop it, but they sure would slow it down

Ideal Husband The guy next door

20

Income Tax   The income tax has made more liars out of the American people than golf has

Indians   I don't blame the Indians for being discouraged. They were the only ones ever to be conquered by the U.S. and not come out ahead

Insurance   Remember, honesty is the best policy—except when trying to collect on your insurance policy

Income   The trouble with marriage is that a fellow can't support a wife and the government on one income

Inflation   When everybody is so rich that no one can afford anything

Inflation   Inflation is when you do more for the dollar than it does for you. Inflation may be hazardous to your wealth

Impossible   There are two things that are really impossible: putting toothpaste back in the tube and getting off a mailing list

Income Tax   The only expense nowadays you can't charge to your credit card

Inflation   Mini money: Inflation has changed things—now one can live as cheaply as two

Inflation   Sign at the Carnegie Deli: "Prices subject to change between courses."

Insurance   The lady sent a letter to the insurance company: "I'm happy to announce that my husband who was reported missing is now definitely dead."

J

Jealousy   I know a guy who didn't kiss his wife for 10 years—then he goes out and shoots a fellow who did

Jogging Thanks to jogging, more people are collapsing in perfect health than ever before

Joint Accounts The lady cried, "My husband accuses me of overdrawing our checking account. I haven't overdrawn—he has under-deposited."

L

Landmarks Some conservation groups are fighting to preserve old buildings in their original form. I know a landlord who's been doing that for years—mine

Lawyer That's a person willing to spend your last cent to prove he's right

Lawyer The man who said talk is cheap never hired a lawyer

Lawyer He's a great lawyer—I got a traffic ticket and he had it reduced to manslaughter

Lawyer A lawyer is a guy who represents you to make sure you get all that's coming to him

Lazy Automation could never replace him. They still haven't invented a machine that does nothing

Liberal A person who makes enemies left and right

Life Red starts off every morning by reading the obituary column: "If I don't see my name—I get out of bed. Then I read a copy of *Playboy* to get my heart started."

Loser Rodney explains it: "My family was so poor—when my rich aunt died, in the will we owed her $100."

LSD Remember when a bad trip was caused by LSD? Now it comes from stopping at the gas station, the supermarket, and the cleaners on the way home

Loser Henry Ford is a loser—with all his money he never owned a Cadillac

Love He always talks to his wife after making love—if she happens to be there

Love I don't know if my wife loves me. Even on our wedding night she told me we were seeing too much of each other

Lonely No man is lonely while eating spaghetti—it takes so much attention

A Loser A sultan who is gay . . . A loser is a guy who would marry Raquel Welch for her money . . . A loser is an accordion player in a topless girl band

Loser Rodney says he's a real loser. "I tell you, since I'm married, I don't worry about bad breath—I never get a chance to open my mouth."

Love and Infatuation Love is blind. Infatuation is when you want to take a second look

Love and Marriage The Gods gave man fire so he put it out with water. They gave him love so he put it out with marriage

M

Marriage Marriage is an institution that teaches a man regularity, frugality, temperance, forbearance, and many other splendid virtues he wouldn't need if he stayed single

Marriage My friend said, "My ambition is to marry a rich girl who is too proud to let her husband work."

Marriage If you really want to know what your girl thinks of you, marry her

Marriage My wife says that she only asked for pin money— but the first pin she wanted had twelve stones in it

Marriage My neighbor explains it: "I'm married to the most perfect woman God ever made—and her mother's even worse."

Marriage is like a cafeteria—you pick out somebody good-looking and pay later . . . Marriage is the only cure for love

Marriage My neighbor says: "Marriage is wonderful—it's my wife I can't stand."

Marriage is a wonderful institution. If it weren't for marriage, husbands and wives would have to fight with perfect strangers

Marriage A lot of people are living together who aren't married—and a lot of people are married who aren't living together

Marriage and Money It is better to marry for money than for no reason at all

Matrimony The wife said, "If you do housework at $100 a week, that's domestic service. If you do it for nothing—that's matrimony."

Medicine House calls are now made only by burglars

Medicine If medical science has made so much progress in the last 10 years—why did I feel so much better 10 years ago?

Medical Convention I attended a medical convention. It's the first time I ever saw pornographic X-rays

Middle Age When a man is warned to slow down by his doctor instead of a policeman

Miser   Nowadays a miser is one who lives within his income

Mistress   Like a wife, only she doesn't have to do the dishes

Modern Mother   Is one who worries when her daughter comes home early from a date

Money   When you have money in your pocket, you are wise and you are handsome and you sing well, too

Money   For the first time in my life I've got money to burn and let's face it—it's cheaper than fuel

Money   Among the things that money can't buy is what it used to

Money   Money can't buy love— but it does put you in a good bargaining position

Money   Jimmy Carter used to say the American dollar was stable—and you know what's found in stables

Mortician   One who covers the doctor's mistakes

Movie Star   The only woman who can keep a maid longer than a husband

Musician   Definition of a true musician: whe he hears a lady singing in the bathtub, he puts his *ear* to the keyhole

N

New Cars   There's a new car on the market that is very cheap if you buy it "as is." But they have about 40 optional extras—one of them is the motor

Nudity   The new things in movies is male nudity. These days the only thing that's being zipped is addresses

Nudist What does a nudist do with his keys after locking his car?

Nympho A nympho has an odd way of stopping a man from making love to her—she simply tires him out

O

Obscene If it's illegal to send obscene material through the mails—how come my electric bill gets through?

Off-Track Betting The OTB now has two windows: fixed races and unfixed races

Old Age That time of life when you don't care where your wife goes, just so you don't have to go with her

Old Age Don't complain about growing old—many people don't have that privilege

Old Age You know you're getting old when all the names in your little black book are doctors

Old Age George Burns says: "Don't try to understand females. By the time you learn to read girls like a book—your library card has expired."

Old Age Is when you know all the answers but nobody asks you the questions

Old Maid A woman who's been good for nothing

Old-Timer One who can remember he used to dream of salaries—that he can't live on today

Old-Timer That's a guy who remembers when sex wasn't a spectator sport

Opportunity Opportunity she knock—but last night knock spoil opportunity

Optimist An optimist says "Fill 'er up" to the gas station attendant, then hands him a $50 bill and waits for change

Optimist An optimist is a man who concludes his wife has given up cigarettes because when he got home from a trip, he found cigar butts all around the house

Optimist and Pessimist If it weren't for the optimist, the pessimist wouldn't know how happy he isn't

Optimist and Pessimist Love is responsible for most of the optimists, and marriage for most of the pessimists

Orator The fellow who is always willing to lay down your life for his country

Orgy Group therapy

P

Panhandler The woman said to the beggar, "I never give money to anyone on the street." The bum said, "What do you want me to do—open an office?"

Dolly Parton I asked Dolly what kind of woman she really is. She said, "Sorry—I can't give out samples."

Patient There's one advantage of being poor—the doctor will cure you faster

Pediatrician and Playboy A pediatrician pats babies on their bare bottoms. A playboy does likewise, but only when they are over 18

A Pessimist   An optimist who voted for a politician who he thought would reduce government spending

Pessimist and Optimist   A pessimist is a man who feels all woman are bad—an optimist hopes so

Philanthropist   One who gives away publicly what he stole privately

Philanthropist   That's a guy who gives away what he should be giving back

Politician   Just got over a terrible case of laryngitis—it was so bad that he could only speak out of one side of his mouth

Politician   Every politician claims he understands the questions of the day. Now if we could find one who understands the answers

Politician   There are two sides to every question—and a good politician takes both

Politics   Give a politician enough rope—and he'll hang you

Politics   America is the only country where you can go on the air and kid politicians and where politicians can go on the air and kid people

Politics   If a politician asks you to vote for him and for good government—you know you'll have to vote twice

Politics   I can't understand why politicians invent lies about each other when the truth could be more damaging . . . The principal advantage of being a defeated candidate is that you don't have to explain why you didn't keep your campaign promises

Politics   What would happen if everybody believed what political candidates say about each other and nobody won?

28

Pollution New York is the only city in the world where mothers call their children in for fresh air

Porno I don't go to porno movies. It's not right to see someone having more fun in an hour than I've had in a lifetime

Post Office If the world is getting smaller why do they keep raising the postal rates?

Post Office You can't blame the I.R.S. for being worried. How would you feel if you had billions of dollars owed you and it was all coming by the U.S. mails?

Practical Nurse One who marries a rich patient

Pregnant The past tense of virgin

Problem Drinkers Are those who never buy

Procurer Fornicaterer

Progress After thousands of years, we have advanced to the point where we bolt our doors and windows, turn on our burglar alarms—while the jungle natives sleep in open-doored huts

Propaganda Baloncy disguised as food for thought

Psychoanalysis The one thing about psychoanalysis is that it prepares you for the poverty in which it leaves you

Psychology The science that tells you what you already know, in words you can't understand

Psychoanalysis Is spending $50 an hour to squeal on your mother

Prude She's such a prude that she blushes when somebody says intersection

R

Radical Anyone whose opinion differs from yours

Radio Announcer A man who talks until you have a headache—and then tries to sell you something to relieve it

Real Estate The real estate agent told the prospective buyer: "Sure we have some $25,000 homes, but it will cost you $100,000."

Rare Steak That's one that costs less than $20

Recession The recession hasn't hurt my family yet—we can still live beyond our means

Reincarnation I definitely believe in reincarnation. Did you ever notice how many dead people come to life every day at five in the afternoon?

Relations Every month I go to Pittsburgh because I have relations there—my wife just found out with whom

Repairman If you can smile when everything goes wrong, you're either an idiot—or a repairman

Restaurants Prices in restaurants are so high—it's wiser to watch your steak than your hat and coat

Retirement Retirement is the time of life when you stop lying about your age and start lying around the house

Robber What a doctor and a plumber call each other

Romance How can you explain romance? He fell in love with a pair of big blue eyes—then made the mistake of marrying the whole girl

Russian Technology "Have you heard the Russians are going to Mars?" "All of them, I hope."

S

Salesmen   An Arab sheik returned home from a vacation in the United States. A fellow sheik asked him: "What impressed you most about the Americans?" "Their salesmen," he replied, strapping on his skis

Sanitation Dept.   I saw this sign on a N.Y.C. garbage truck: "If you are not satisfied with our methods you will receive double your garbage back."

Savings   A penny saved—isn't worth the effort

Savoir Faire   Three men were discussing savoir faire. One said, "If I go home and find my wife kissing another man and say 'Excuse me' that is savoir faire." The second said, "Not quite. If I come home and find my wife kissing another man and say, 'Excuse me—please continue' that's savoir faire." The third said, "If I come home and find my wife kissing another man and I say 'Excuse me—please continue' and he *can* continue *that's* savoir fair."

School Days   School days are the best days of your life—provided your children are old enough to go

Senior Citizens   I went to a social at a senior citizens club. It was the first time I drank a martini with a prune in it

Sex   At his age, his idea of wild sex is being frisked by a lady guard at the airport

Sex   For those of you who can't give up sex—get married and taper off

Sex   There are a lot of things I don't understand. Like Dr. Reuben's book, *Everything You Wanted to Know about Sex.* The only thing is, he left out the most important part—where to get it

Sex The battle of the sexes will never be won by either side—there is too much fraternizing with the enemy

Sex There are so many sex magazines on the stands today—I'm taking a course in speed looking

Sex Just when you think you know everything about sex another expert comes along with a new book

Sex The husband asked, "How come you never tell me when you enjoy sex?" She answered, "Because you're never home."

Sex There are better things than sex and there are worse things—but nothing quite like it . . . Never make love when you have something better to do. But what's better?

Sign of Success When it costs more to support the government than it does your family

Silver With the price of silver today—people would stand in line to be shot by the Lone Ranger

Ski-Jumping That's a leap made by a person on the way to the hospital . . You race down a steep hill and fly hundreds of feet into the air. Now, there must be a better way to meet nurses

Snob A snob is a person who only wants to know the people who don't want to know him

Specialist That's a doctor whose patients can be ill only during office hours

Spending My neighbor accused his wife of spending money like a drunken sailor. She answered, "Is that any worse than spending like a sober Congressman?"

Socialized Medicine When women get together and talk about their operations

Society This society playboy (in a small town he'd be known as the town drunk)—the only thing he did for a living is read his father's will—looked down at Mr. Cohen and sneered, "One of my ancestors signed the Declaration of Independence." "So?" Mr. Cohen answered. "One of mine signed the Ten Commandments."

St. Patrick St. Patrick chased the snakes out of Ireland—now, if someone will only chase the baboons out of Congress.

Statesman That's a politician who didn't get caught

Stockbroker A man who is always ready to back his judgment with your last dollar

Stock Market Investor He is someone who is alert, informed, attuned to the economic heartbeat of America, and cries a lot

Strip Teaser A busy body

Suburbs To live in the country, one must have the soul of a poet, the mind of a philosopher, the simple taste of a hermit, and a good station wagon

Suburbanite A suburbanite is a man who hires someone to cut the grass so he can play golf for the exercise

Subways This kid was explaining the subway system in New York: "Parents say the subway system is not safe in New York. So they put 1,800 cops in the subways. I was on the subway on my way to school and I got up to give my seat to a woman—and a cop grabbed it."

Success Many a man owes his success to his first wife and his second wife to his success

Success Success is making more money so you can pay off the taxes you wouldn't have to pay if you didn't have so much money already

Success   Success is relative. The more success, the more relatives

Sympathy   What one usually gives to a friend or relative, when he doesn't want to lend him money

T

Tax Audit   "Where seldom is heard an encouraging word . . .

Tax Collectors and Psychiatrists   Tax collectors and psychiatrists are giving out the same advice—it's not good for a man to keep too much to himself

Taxes   The American public owes a lot to the I.R.S.—ulcers, nausea, diarrhea

Taxes   Only in a democracy have the citizens complete freedom in deciding to pay their taxes—by check, cash, or money order

Taxes   Patrick Henry should come back to see what taxation *with* representation is like

Taxes   When a Congressman says he's for a tax cut—it simply means he wants his cut of your taxes

Taxes   All the taxes paid over a lifetime by the average American family are spent by the government in less than a second

Tax Loopholes   Are like parking spaces—they all seem to disappear by the time you get there

Taxpayer   The biggest job Congress has is how to get the money from the taxpayer without disturbing the voter

Teenagers   Children grow up so quickly—one day you look at the phone bill and realize they're teenagers

Television TV helps you get acquainted with a lot of new people—mostly repairmen

Television The greatest spectacle of the year was my TV repairman's bill

Television Permits you to be entertained in your living room by characters you wouldn't ordinarily allow in your living room

Television Movies on television are just like furniture—they're either early American or old English

Tightwad One who has an impediment in his reach

Topless Bar That's where you can always find a friendly face—and nobody watching it

Traffic One way to stop traffic jams is to allow on the streets only the automobiles that have been paid for

Travel After seeing those backward broken-down countries it's good to be back in New York and see those broken-down streets

Travel Brings something into your life you never had before: poverty

Travel Travel is broadening—especially if you stop at all the recommended eating places . . . You can't take it with you—but that's not true when my wife travels

Troubles Take your troubles like a man—blame them on your wife

U

Undertaker One who follows the medical profession

Unions In unions there is strength and in unions more strength . . . every child born in America has two strikes against it—at least Rodney told his son, "Learn a trade so you'll be able to go out on strike."

United Nations Is made up of countries that cannot tolerate injustice and oppression—except at home

Used Cars The best way to buy a used car is when it's new

Untouchables People who won't give charity. The girl approached the businessman and asked, "Would you donate to the sexual freedom league?" He said, "I give at home."

W

Wall Street You must look at the positive side of Wall Street—like the sound, secure investments of today are the tax losses of tomorrow

Warden The only man who should not be judged by the company he keeps

George Washington If George knew how little you can buy with a dollar these days—he probably wouldn't want his picture on it

Raquel Welch "I see you're a man with ideals—I guess I better be going while you've still got them."

Wife If you think you have trouble supporting your wife— just try not supporting her

Wife Picking out a wife is like buying a new tie. It always looks better when you're picking it out than when it's home and around your neck

Wife The man who holds the car door open for his wife has either a new wife or a new car

Wolf He's got a good head on his shoulders—but it's a different one every night

Wolf A wolf is the kind of guy who doesn't care if a girl's head is empty—as long as her blouse is full

Work Work is something that when we have it, we wish we didn't; when we don't have it, we wish we did; and the object of most of it is to be able to afford not to do any some day

Women's Lib My neighbor explains it all: "I'm glad my wife joined women's lib. Now she complains about *all* men, not just me."

Women's Lib Too many girls get married before they can adequately support a husband

Work People are still willing to do an honest day's work— only they want a week's pay for it

Institutions: Romance, Marriage, Mothers-in-law, Cheating, & Divorce

"Romance just ain't the same anymore," my nephew complained. "I asked one girl to be my valentine—she said she'd have to discuss it with her attorney." Girls these days defy the law of gravity. They're easier to pick up than drop . . . Now I understand that Linda Ronstadt has sued Jerry Brown for half of California.

The unwed mother was in the hospital nursing her illegitimate child when the doctor entered. "Your hair is red," said the doctor, "but the child's hair is brown. What was the color of the father's hair?" The mother said, "I really don't know— he didn't take his hat off."

"Dear Frankie," the loving letter began, "I haven't been able to sleep ever since I broke our engagement. Won't you forget and forgive? Your absence leaves a void nobody else could ever fill. I love you, I need you, I want you. Your loving Marian. P.S. Congratulations on winning the million dollar lottery."

Rodney Dangerfield is also unlucky in love: "My wife wants her sex in the back seat of a car—and she wants *me* to drive . . ." Rodney admits he gets no respect anyplace. He was making love to a girl and she started to cry. He asked gently, "Will you hate yourself in the morning?" She said, "No—I hate myself *now*."

As a kid, Rodney had a lot of charisma. Then he started dating girls and his charisma cleared up. . . . "I had problems from the beginning," Rodney admits. "When I was engaged to my wife, I wanted a big wedding—and she wanted to call the whole thing off . . ." He says, "Do you realize we are living in the midst of the world's greatest sexual revolution? What do you want to bet that I end up on the losing side?"

Two pretty actresses were discussing the merits of a young off-Broadway producer. "He's such a sharp and attractive dresser," said one. The other admitted, "Yes—and so quickly, too."

The beautiful young actress was confiding to a friend. "He tried everything—flowers, candy, jewelry, furs—and they all worked."

The new secretary looked easy, so he put the pressure on: "If you have no plans for the weekend," the boss said, "Why don't you come to my summer place; we'll have some fun." She smiled. "Okay—and I'll bring my boyfriend." He said, "Your boyfriend? What the hell for?" She said, "In case your wife wants to have some fun, too."

Advice to the loveworn: When wine, women, and song become too much for you—give up singing.

The 65-year-old man who had just married a girl less than half his age went to his doctor for a checkup. "Do you think I'm overweight?" he asked after the examination. The doc said, "No—just overmatched."

"I had everything a man could want," the poor soul groaned. "Money, a gorgeous home, the love of a beautiful and wealthy woman. Then suddenly one morning my wife walked in."

The clerk was on his honeymoon and sent a cable to his employer saying, "It's wonderful here—please extend my leave another week." The boss returned the message immediately: "It's wonderful anywhere—come home at once!"

"What do you do if you love a rich man and a poor man, each for different reasons?" the girl asked her parents. "Simple," mom said, "I'd marry the rich man—and be good to the poor."

She said, "You want to marry me? But you've only known me three days." Lover Boy said, "Oh, much longer than that. I've worked two years in the bank where your father has his account."

Woody Allen talks about love: "After six years of marriage, my wife and I couldn't decide whether to take a vacation or get a divorce. We decided that a trip to Bermuda is over in two weeks—but a divorce is something you always have."

Remember, you promised to take her for "better or for worse." Years ago, a woman cooked for you, cleaned for you, and sewed for you. Today when a woman says "I do," that's the last thing she does.

It happens I love my wife but she is a bit extravagant—she tips at toll booths. She said to me: "All right, I love to spend money—but you just name me one other extravagance."

Lem was so shy but he finally asked Sue for a date and they went horseback riding. When they stopped the two horses began nuzzling each other affectionately and Lem said wistfully, "Now that's what I'd like to do," and Sue said, "Go ahead—it's your horse."

My neighbor's wife said to him, "Darling, of course I spend more than you make—but that's only because I have such confidence in you!"

Stop praising a woman and she thinks you don't love her anymore; keep it up and she thinks she's too good for you.

There is only one way to handle a woman. The trouble is—nobody knows what it is.

Love at first sight saves a lot of time and money. Love is blind and marriage an eye-opener.

The young lady asked Zsa Zsa if she thought a girl should get married for love. Zsa answered, "Yes, I do—and she should keep getting married until she finds it."

The husband told the judge that he wanted a divorce because his wife called him a lousy lover. "You want a divorce because your wife called you a lousy lover?" He said, "No—I want a divorce because she knows the difference."

"How come you stopped drinking, smoking, gambling, and sexing?" I asked my neighbor. "Because my girl asked me to," he explained. "So how come you didn't marry her?" He said, "Well, since I'm such a clean-cut, decent, desirable man now I figured I could do a lot better than her."

After only six dates, the girl's mother announced, "My daughter is getting married—and I hope she'll make her husband as happy as she's making my husband."

Kevin Goldstein-Jackson says: "When I was in my 20s I went crazy over a girl. For a long time we had a love-hate relationship. I loved her—she hated me. This was probably due to our religious differences: I was broke and she worshipped money." Kevin admits, "It was very difficult for me to get married—I had an enormous problem finding someone who loved me as much as I did."

Divorce has become a national institution . . . They even have whole professions springing up around it. For instance, did you ever hear of a *marriage* lawyer? . . . To show how things are speeding up: In Hollywood, I just heard of a film star who started divorce proceedings, three weeks *before* her wedding . . . "I want to find out if I have grounds for divorce," the man asked the divorce lawyer. "Are you married?" the lawyer asked. "Why yes, of course," the client replied. "Then you have grounds."

Many couples break up because it looks like the marriage is going to last forever . . . One Hollywood marriage I know didn't work out—everywhere they went they kept running into each other . . . My neighbor and his wife are getting a divorce because of arithmetic—she put two and two together . . . I think my best friend's marriage is on the rocks—I understand for their anniversary they got his and her lawyers.

A Broadway playboy was rejoicing over the terms of his recently granted divorce: "My ex-wife got the car, the dog, the house, and custody of the four kids—I didn't get stuck with anything . . ." My brother's wife says that if he ever divorced her, he can have the kids. Not only that, but if she ever has any more kids—he gets them, too.

"What would it take for you to go on a second honeymoon?" she asked. "A second wife," he answered . . . "And there's the guy who divorced his wife because she was always complaining about the housework—she didn't like the way he did it . . . Two Hollywood starlets were discussing their boyfriends. "My new fella," said one, "is a perfect dream. He doesn't drink, gamble, or even as much as look at another girl." The other cried, "Gosh, how will you ever get a divorce?"

There's a famous Hollywood couple who won't get a divorce until their son passes his bar exams—they want to be his first case . . . Then there's the sentimental Hollywood star who wanted to get divorced in the same dress in which her mother got divorced.

The sexy wife of a busy husband won a divorce recently, charging her hubby with lack of attentiveness. "If anything ever happened to me," the stacked missus complained, "my husband wouldn't be able to identify the body . . ." Another bitter wife exclaimed, "I'd divorce him—if I could find a way to do it without making him happy."

Alimony keeps matrimony from being a failure . . . As one man put it, "Tis better to have loved and received alimony than never to have loved at all . . ." As the man said when his rich wife offered to pay off: "Love has its compensations, and they are usually called alimony . . ." Many a man falls behind in his alimony payments because his second wife doesn't earn as much as he had expected.

"Alimony is something that enables a man to profit by his mistakes," says the male chauvinist pig. "It's a man's cash-surrender value. If we are going to have women's lib it should apply equally, and alimony is a system by which when two people make a mistake, one of them continues to pay for it—man or woman."

My neighbor's wife explains it very well: "Now that I'm working, I not only understand economics but can explain it very well: a recession is when your neighbor loses his job; a depression is when you lose your job; a panic is when your wife loses her job . . ." "Being a career woman," says my aunt, "is harder than being a career man. You've got to look like a lady, act like a man, and work like a dog."

My uncle cried, "Then there's my first wife. I couldn't live with that woman after what she said to me. She said, 'Get out and stay out . . .'" My neighbor says, "You know your marriage is in trouble when you get dressed in the dark and you find yourself wearing the mailman's pants."

Morris was awakened out of his sleep at 4 A.M. by his wife who said, "If I were to die would you get married again?" "Wh-a-at kind of a question at this time of the morning," he mumbled. "Would you get married again?" she insisted. "Yeah," he admitted. "I suppose so—eventually." "Would you bring her to live here in this house?" "This is a ridiculous conservation," he protested drowsily, "but it's a nice house, why shouldn't we live here?" "Would you give her my car?" The husband yawned. "Why not? It's a BMW and it's less than a year old. Yeah. I'd give her your car." The wife pushed on. "What about my golf clubs?" "No," Morris said firmly, "Your golf clubs I wouldn't give her." "Why not?" she asked. "Because," the husband said, "She's left-handed."

46

Let's look at the wife's side for a change. The wife said, "I'm wearing my new dresses shorter this year." The husband said, "I'd like it better if you wore the old ones a little longer . . ." One husband was raving, "We got along just great for six years. Then she decided to come back home."

This gentleman went to a marriage bureau and tried to find himself a wife. "You needn't be too fussy," he explained, "I only want her for wife-swapping parties."

An executive arrived home at 8 one morning and told his wife he had been up much of the night at an important conference. When the conference ended, he had to drive his secretary home. She asked him in for a cup of coffee and put him up for the remainder of the night because it was so late . . . His wife listened to his explanation with suspicion. "Don't lie to me," she cried, "I know you were playing cards at the club again."

My neighbor's wife said, "I am completely opposed to divorce. I just don't like the idea of sharing my husband's money with a lawyer."

The California community property laws are easily explained. After you split with them—they want to split with you.

Marriage vows should be changed to fit the crime: Actor: "Do you promise to love, honor, and applaud?" Businessman: "Until debt do us part . . ." "The secret of a happy marriage," she told her husband, "is in doing things together —like opening a joint bank account."

Research at Florida State University dealt with how married women prefer to spend their leisure time. Sex came in second, way behind reading and barely ahead of sewing! And though many women said they DO enjoy sex, some indicated they enjoy it MORE while reading or sewing.

A man called the undertaker and cried, "Come over and bury my wife . . ." "But," said the mortician, "I buried your wife ten years ago . . ." "I got married again," sobbed the man. "Congratulations," said the undertaker.

My neighbor's wife is depressed. She took one of those *Cosmopolitan* quizzes: "Is your mate a passionate lover?" Not only did it show he wasn't passionate, it also showed that for the past three years he'd been dead.

Marriage is coming back. The headlines say 2.2 million marriages were performed last year, making it the best year for wedlock since 1970 . . . My neighbor got the spirit and decided to marry his live-in lady . . . "I feel like Zsa Zsa's next husband," he said. "I know what to do, but how do you make it interesting?" . . . Zsa Zsa made a real success of marriage—she was the first one to do it as a series.

"Marriage is beautiful," the Hollywood actor noted. "My wife and I have been working together, planning together, and saving together, just so that we could do something that we've always wanted to do—get a divorce . . ." My uncle was telling his bar pals: "My wife and I have finally achieved sexual compatibility—last night we both had a headache . . ." My friend's wife is a gypsy. The other night she was reading her crystal ball and her husband tried to get a little affectionate. She pushed him aside and said, "Not tonight— I'm going to have a headache."

Rodney admits that his marriage is a bit shaky: "The other night my wife told me to take out the garbage. I told her I already took out the garbage and she told me to go out and keep an eye on it . . ." Rodney says, "I first suspected the thrill was gone when my wife suggested taking a second honeymoon—by herself."

Two women were talking about their husbands. One said: "I'm more and more convinced that mine married me for my money." The other said, "Then you have the satisfaction of knowing that he's not as stupid as he looks."

The large number of divorces indicates that America is still the land of the free. Sure, but the increasing marriage rate shows that it's still the home of the brave.

Statistics prove that 50% of all the married couples in the world today are husbands. Today we hear from the little man. Which is probably the first time he has had a chance to open his mouth since he said "I do . . ." "The best way to support a wife these days," says one poor soul, "is to send her off to work." Another says: "Behind every successful man stands a wife with a handful of bills."

"You beast, you animal," she screamed, "I'm going back to mother." He said, "Never mind—I'll go back to my wife . . ." The only way she can get money out of her husband is to tell him she's going home to her mother. He then immediately gives her a couple of hundred dollars for plane fare . . .

Your marriage is in trouble when your wife introduces Masters and Johnson as her best friends . . . You are having a problem when you check into your honeymoon hotel and your wife asks for a room with instructions . . . "I've got a couple of wonderful seats tonight, darling," the husband said, "yours is for the opera and mine is for the fights."

Something has gone out of the marriage when he starts wondering what happened to the girl he married and she starts wondering what happened to the man she didn't . . . He said, "Well, it finally happened. There's a monthly installment due every day." She said, "Perhaps we could borrow a little each month and set that aside." He said, "Dear, if we continue to save at our present rate—at retirement we will owe $300,000 . . ."

My aunt just had her 12th child and she's running out of names—to call her husband . . . "This is my third marriage," the lady told Zsa Zsa. Zsa said, "Good—keep trying till you get it right . . ." Zsa Zsa and Liz have been married seven times each. One more time and they'll be listed in the yellow pages.

Like the widow said to the bachelor: "Take it from me—don't get married."

I'm tired of the comics making jokes about marriage. Henny Youngman says, "Take my wife—*PLEASE*—Man is not complete until he's married—then he's finished. . ." Milton Berle cries, "That last word in an argument is what the wife says. Anything a husband says after that is the beginning of another argument. . ." Morey Amsterdam claims his wife is very cooperative: "I told her there was a button missing on my coat—so she sewed up the hole."

I think we should listen to the wife's side for a change. This new bride in my building is convinced her honeymoon is over. The other night while watching TV the couple saw a passionate love scene. She turned to her husband and asked, "Why don't you ever make love to me like that?" He said, "Do you have any idea how much they pay that fellow?"

I am a romantic. I want to hear about happy couples. William B. Williams says, "Actually, my wife and I are very romantic—we won't even argue except by candlelight . . ." Red Buttons told me, "For our last anniversary, I asked my wife which she'd prefer, a mink or a trip to Sweden?" She said, "Let's go to Sweden, it's cheaper there."

Let's not fight. Like this guy who antagonized his wife with the same words every night when he went out: "Good night— mother of three." One night she could stand it no longer. When he put his hat on and started for the door he said cheerily, "Good night—mother of three." She answered gaily, "Good night—father of one."

The husband asked his wife angrily, "Another new hat! Another new fur! Where will I get the money to pay for it?" She answered, "Whatever my faults, dear, I'm not inquisitive . . ." "Maybe money can't buy happiness," her friend told her, "but it makes misery more comfortable." She said, "Girls don't marry a man for his money—they divorce him for it."

50

"Marriage is like a friendship that somehow got out of control," says Jan Murray . . . Joan Rivers notes, "For fixing things around the house, nothing beats a man who's handy with a checkbook."

Everybody is knocking marriage these days. I'd like to look at the brighter side . . . There are as many girls looking for husbands as there are husbands looking for girls . . . Every woman needs a man because there are some things that go wrong that you can't blame on the government.

My neighbor was telling a friend that his wife is no longer jealous. "You see," he explained, "I turn all the money I earn over to her. She figures that if I can get anything for free at my age—I'm entitled."

Perfect mates come only in shoes and gloves . . . The wife said, "If you really loved me, you would have married someone else . . ." She said, "Before we got married, you told me you were well off." He said, "I was and I didn't know it."

My neighbor was complaining, "Every week my wife acts like she's at the Academy Awards. When I come home from work she says, 'Envelope, please.'"

She was not feeling well, so she went to see her doctor. After an examination and some questions, he said, "There's nothing really the matter with you. All you need is sex once a day every day . . ." That night she told her husband what the doctor had prescribed. "Okay," said her husband. "Put me down for Mondays and Thursdays."

Goldstein the marriage broker called on Sylvia and announced that he had found the ideal husband for her—a black belt at karate and the quickest draw in the East. "There's only one problem," the matchmaker said, "I told him you are a rich lady, but he insists business is business and he wants you to give him a sample of your sexual ability." She snapped, "Well, you go right back and tell him I know a little about business. Samples I'm not giving him—references I'll give him."

As far as I'm concerned, I think all marriages are happy—it's the living together afterwards that causes the trouble . . . Like the man who advertised for a wife in the paper. He got 1,800 replies from men who said he could have theirs . . . Or my friend Arthur, who was known for the punctuality with which he sent his wife her alimony payments each month. When asked the reason for his haste he shivered and explained, "I'm afraid that if I ever should fall behind in my payments, she might decide to repossess me."

I asked John Travolta if he believes in love and marriage. He said, "Yes, but not necessarily with the same person . . ." Robert Redford says, "My wife and I are at the age where we're still ready, willing, and able—but seldom all three at the same time."

"Have you heard?" my neighbor said. "Many couples are now experimenting with a life style that involves living together without sex—it's called marriage!"

A lawyer met a client who was about to be married. "I'd like to congratulate you," he said, "you will always look back on this day as the happiest in your life." The man replied, "Thank you—but it's tomorrow that I'm to be married." The lawyer said, "Yes—I know that."

She said, "I can no longer trust my husband, he is so deceitful. He pretends to believe me when he knows I'm lying to him . . ." She was nagging him as usual. "This is the last straw," she threatened, "I'm going to divorce you." Her long-suffering mate smiled weakly. "Now, dear," he murmured, "I know you don't mean it—you're just saying it to make me feel good."

At the marriage counselor's, the husband accused his wife of being frigid. She screamed, "That's not true. I don't disapprove of sex relations—but this sex fiend expects it every month."

Zsa Zsa Gabor was bragging on television the other night that she had seven husbands, "They all beat me up and I loved it." How can you explain romance? Zsa Zsa never cared for a man's company—unless he owned it. She told me one time about her two boyfriends. "If I could combine their good qualities, I'd be the happiest girl in the world. Frank is smart, debonair, rich and handsome, and has a lot of money besides, and Martin wants to marry me."

The father said to the groom-to-be: "So, my daughter has consented to become your wife. Have you fixed the day of the wedding?" He said, "I will leave that to my fiancée." The father asked, "And will you have a church or a private wedding?" He answered, "Her mother will decide that, sir." Pop asked, "What will you have to live on?" The groom said, "I will leave that entirely to you, sir."

The young man finally summoned up enough courage to ask the girl's father for his daughter's hand in marriage . . . "I'll have to think about it for a while," said the stern old father. "And I'm sure I needn't remind you that whoever marries my daughter gets a rare and beautiful prize." "Oh, really?" the boy said, brightening up. "How's chances of seeing it now!"

Charlie was scolding his younger brother who had just dropped out of college: "Every time I see you, you're either drunk or running around with wild broads—or both. Don't you know what good clean fun is?" The kid brother answered, "No—what good is it?"

Frances was in a dither. Her new fella's birthday was coming up and she couldn't think of what to give him. She asked gramma: "You know how rich he is; he drives a Rolls, and has a yacht, a town house, a country estate, mink-lined shoes, diamond watches, jeweled cigarette cases, platinum electric shavers—what can a girl give a man who has everything?" Wise old grandma said, "Encouragement, dearie, encouragement."

Bertha loved Charlie, even if he was 80. He had a will of his own and she was a beneficiary, but he was always screaming, "Sex is too high—sex is too high." Finally she asked him,

"What do you mean sex is too high?" And the old man said, "It's all up here in my head."

The big Wall Street executive held the voluptuous blonde very close and whispered, "I love you, darling, as no one has ever loved before." She said, "I can't see any difference."

I'm retiring these jokes to the hall of fun. Like the one about the judge who said gravely to the woman on the witness stand, "So, you deceived your husband?" She answered, "On the contrary, your Honor, he deceived me. He said he was going out of town and he didn't go."

Tired of being a widower, farmer Smith went into town, picked out a wife, married her, turned his horse around and drove homeward. The horse stumbled. "That's once," said the farmer. A little later, the horse stumbled again. "That's twice," said the farmer. When the horse stumbled again, he said, "That's three times," and pulled out his gun and shot the horse dead. "You heartless brute!" screamed his bride, slapping him across the face. He looked at her for a moment and said, "That's once . . ."

My neighbor says he doesn't mind his wife going through his pockets while he's asleep—what bothers him is the way she goes through his bank account while he's awake.

Charlie said to his wife: "Let's go out and have some fun this evening." She said, "Great idea—and if you get home before me, don't bolt the front door."

The woman accused her husband of cheating. "What would you do if you came home and found me making love to another man?" she cried. "Do? I would break his white stick and chase his seeing-eye dog."

A recent study indicates that more and more unmarried couples are living together these days. That isn't right. They don't know what life is all about until they have endured the agonies of wedded bliss.

Phyllis Diller's advice to brides: "Burn the toast so he won't notice the coffee."

She gave the detective $5,000 and explained, "My husband is having an affair with a redhead. I want you to follow them 24 hours a day—and then I want you to come and tell me what she sees in him."

My neighbor complained: "My wife is a girl who 25 years ago said 'I do' and then never did."

Statistics in the U.S.A. are very depressing about marriage. They say that one out of every three marriages ends in divorce—the other two end in murder.

What do I know? I thought *Star Wars* was about a Hollywood divorce court.

She asked her husband naively, "Does money talk, dear?" He said, "That's what they say." She said, "Well I wish you would leave some here to talk to me during the day—I get so lonely."

The bride sulked, "I'm sick of marriage—Charlie hasn't kissed me since I came back from my honeymoon." The friend asked, "Then why don't you divorce him?" She said, "Oh I'm not married to Charlie."

My wife is kind of naive. I bought her a copy of *The Joy of Sex* and she thought it was a cookbook. You should see what she serves me for dinner.

I never forget my wife's birthday. I just forget which one it is. Cindy gave me very simple instructions for buying her birthday present: "If you can afford it—forget it."

Here's how the great rate their mate: "It takes two to make a marriage—a bride and her mother"-Bob Hope. "The formula for a successful marriage is the same I have always used for making cars—stick to one model"-Henry Ford. "Husbands are like fires—they go out when unattended."-Zsa Zsa Gabor. "Marriage is like a warm bath—once you get used to it, it's not so hot"-Phyllis Diller.

Milton Berle says, "There are two good reasons why my marriage has lasted so long. First, my wife and I go out every weekend. Second, she doesn't ask me where I go and I don't aske her where she goes."

Phyllis Diller says: "The closest I ever came to suicide is marriage. On our honeymoon my husband swore he wouldn't drink while working—and he hasn't touched a job since."

No wonder there are so many unhappy marriages: the best man never gets the bride . . . Zsa and Liz claim: "Every girl waits for the right man to come along—but in the meantime she gets married."

A fool and his money are soon married . . . She said: "My timing is bad. If I had married him a year ago, I'd be divorced by now."

My neighbor says: "My wife meets me halfway on everything. It's my house, she lives in it; it's my car, she drives it; it's my money, she spends it. She's only waiting for me to have a nervous breakdown so she can go to Florida."

She was bragging about what a great wife she is: "After I married my husband he became a millionaire." I asked what he was before she married him. She said, "A multi-millionaire."

They met on a blind date, and it ripened into friendship—then it rotted into marriage. You can always tell when a marriage is shaky. The partners don't even talk during television commercials.

One teenage marriage in the Village broke up so fast, they're still fighting over who gets custody of the wedding cake.

Pop told his daughter that the young man from the bank asked for her hand in marriage and he consented. She said, "But Daddy, I hate to leave mother." He said, "That's perfectly okay, dear, just take her with you!"

There's a lot to be said about marriage—but who has the nerve?

When I was a kid I read about the Moslems and others who were allowed many wives. "How come?" I asked my father. "Why, a man in America is not allowed more than one wife." He said, "Son, when you're older you'll realize that the law protects those who are not capable of protecting themselves."

After the court awarded the woman a large marital settlement, she met her husband in the corridor. She said, "I want you to know I always had your best interests at heart." He hollered, "Then why the hell did you marry me?"

Love sickness can usually be cured by marriage—which you have to admit is pretty drastic medicine.

Henny Youngman raved to me: "Isn't this electronic world we are living in great? Right now my wife is home taping an argument with me!"

I saw the weirdest thing at a Hollywood wedding—even the two little figures on top of the cake were arguing.

Marriage is the only cure for love. Myron Cohen says, "All these 50 years I've been married I have never thought of divorce—murder, yes."

"Television is helping keep my marriage together," says Claire Windsor. "TV is so dull this year we may have a population explosion. Men are actually talking to their own wives."

My neighbor's wife called her mother and cried that she had a fight with him. She wanted to come to her house. Her mother said, "How will that punish him?—I'll come to your house."

The other day my neighbor was complaining about his wife. "Joey, I'm worried. She spends a lot of time talking to flowers." I said, "So what? A lot of people talk to flowers." He said, "When they're in wallpaper?"

There is one thing more exasperating than a wife who can cook and won't—and that's a wife who can't cook and will.

Today men don't ask their wives "What's cooking?" They ask "What's thawing?"

Pat Henry says: "I really don't complain too much when my wife serves me those TV dinners. But I do get a little annoyed when she starts heating up the leftovers and calls them reruns."

My wife does wonderful things with leftovers—she throws them out.

My neighbor is such a lousy cook. Her husband is so thin, when he holds his hands over his head he looks like a fork. He admits she isn't such a good cook: "We had people for dinner two weeks ago—and they're still sitting there."

We got a new cook at home and she's a gem. Chicken, turkey, roast beef, you name it. It makes no difference to her. She eats everything.

My wife and I have found a simple, yet effective way to stay within our food budget—it's called starvation.

The wife was screaming, "What do you mean by coming home half drunk?" He answered, "I ran out of money."

Some husbands maintain they deserve at least one night off each week. Mr. Finkelstein was one of these, and what's more, he convinced Mrs. Finkelstein of the merit of his position. So every Friday, regular as clockwork, he would hop into his car and join the boys at the local bar for a drink or two. One day he didn't come home and he was gone for seven years. Then, one Friday evening, he returned as suddenly as he had disappeared. Mrs. Finkelstein was so happy to see him that she called up her friends to come and celebrate. "Wait just a minute," objected Mr. Finkelstein. "What do you think you're doing?" "Just having a few friends over in honor of your return," said Mrs. Finkelstein. "What?" growled Finkelstein. "On my night out?"

The honeymoon is over when a quickie before dinner means a cocktail . . . The honeymoon is over when he phones he'll be late again for dinner and she has already left a note that it's in the refrigerator . . . The honeymoon was over when he told her she reminded him of Catherine the Great, the great lover. She said sweetly, "Really? Why?" He said, "For one thing, she's been dead for years."

Charles was 93 and Myrtle was 91. They were married in a beautiful ceremony on the first of June—and they spent the first 2 days of their honeymoon trying to get out of the car.

The young woman went to a fortune teller who said, "You will soon meet a tall, handsome man who will sweep you off your feet. He will shower you with gifts and take you to exotic places on your honeymoon." She asked, "Is he rich?" The fortune teller said, "He is president of a bank and is loaded." The girl said, "Gee, can you tell me one more thing? How can I get rid of my husband?"

The Hollywood mother was advising her daughter before the ceremony: "Don't worry, dear. Mother will tell you everything you should know before you get married." The bride shrieked, "That's wonderful! Then I'll be able to get as much alimony as you did."

The salesman had a stateroom on the train, but he was lonesome and went out into the coach and sat down beside an attractive girl. "Are you married?" he asked. She said, "Yes, are you?" He admitted he was. Finally they went to enjoy in the privacy of his stateroom. Later when the conductor opened the door and found them entwined like a pretzel, the salesman said, "It's okay—we're married."

Two expectant fathers were pacing nervously up and down the corridor of the hospital waiting room. "Why did this have to happen on the first day of my vacation?" one complained. The other said, "*You* should complain?—This is our honeymoon!"

My friend was saying, "Going to a party with your wife is like going fishing with the game warden . . ." He was celebrating his 25th wedding anniversary and gave a big party for his friends, but he sat in his bedroom by himself getting loaded. I found him and asked why he was so sad instead of celebrating with his pals. He explained, "When I had been married for five years I decided to kill my wife. I went to a lawyer and told him what I was going to do. He said that if I did it I could get twenty years in prison. Just think, tonight I could have been a free man."

It's easy these days to tell if a man is married. All you have to do is watch when he opens his wallet. If he turns his back while doing it, he's married.

I met a friend in the lobby of the Hilton in Hong Kong. "My wife is an hour late," he growled. "She's either been kidnapped, hit by a motor car, or she's shopping—I hope she hasn't been shopping."

We have holidays for everything and everybody but never mothers-in-law. It's about time we honored them instead of knocking them. My beautiful mother-in-law has been living with Cindy and me since we got married 27 years ago. And she can live with us forever. What can I do—it's her apartment.

It was the peak of a quarrel and the wife turned to the husband and shrieked, "If only I had taken my mother's advice—I never would have married you!" The husband stopped in his tracks. "Do you mean to tell me that your

60

mother tried to keep you from marrying me?" The wife barked, "She certainly did." The husband moaned, "Oh, how I've wronged that woman."

A husband, worried by a fall-off in his business, suggested for the time being that his wife fire the maid and do a little housework herself. "I think you're the one who's going to have to fire her," pointed out the wife. "After all, she's your mother."

One guy I know divorced his wife and married her sister— he didn't want to break in a new mother-in-law . . . Remember, be nice to your mother-in-law—it's cheaper than hiring a baby-sitter . . . "I don't mind my mother-in-law living with us," my neighbor told me, "but at least she could have waited until we got married."

I met a friend who told me he was taking his mother-in-law to Alaska for a vacation. I asked, "Won't the weather disagree with her?" He said, "It wouldn't dare."

I often wondered what happens to that sweet little old mother when she becomes a mother-in-law . . . As Cindy says, "Love is blind—but your mother-in-law isn't."

"Why is it you hate all my relatives?" the wife cried. He said, "Now, that's not true—you know I like your mother-in-law a lot better than mine . . ." The only thing a divorce proves is whose mother was right in the first place.

A hundred years ago a woman called to her mate who was up a tree: "There's a ferocious tiger gone into the cave where my mother is. Do something!" He answered, "Why should I care what happens to the tiger?"

Revolutionary comic Lenny Bruce once remarked that he objected to mother-in-law jokes. Even though, "My mother-in-law did break up my marriage. My wife came home from work one day and found me making love to her."

Jan Murray says, "I just got back from a pleasure trip—I took my mother-in-law to the airport . . ." Milton Berle complains, "I told my mother-in-law, 'My house is your house' so last week she sold it . . ." Soupy Sales explains, "I got this bottle of Scotch for my mother-in-law—not a bad exchange."

The newlywed said to his wife: "Now I realize why you married me—just to give your mother another man to criticize . . ." The woman said to her neighbor, "If you dislike your daughter's boyfriend so much why do you want them to get married?" She answered, "I'm just looking forward to being that young man's mother-in-law."

Sixty percent of the men cheat in America—the rest cheat in Europe.

Ever since Bing Crosby introduced *Love Thy Neighbor*, cheating has become Long Island's favorite pastime. My neighbor told me he just hired a detective to watch his wife: "Not that she's unfaithful—I just want to know where she is when I am."

The Broadway show *The Cheaters* brought it all out in the open. Lou Jacobi screamed, "That dirty rat sweetheart of mine," he said about his girl. "That cheat. She's been married all along and I never knew it until my wife told me."

The wife found her husband with her girl friend. The argument was hot and heavy. "Let's play gin for him," the girl suggested when they couldn't find a solution. "If I lose, I give him up. If you lose, you give him up." The wife answered, "Well, to make it more interesting—let's play for a penny a point."

I know a guy who's been wearing a girdle for three months— ever since his wife found it in the glove compartment of his car. She had her own alibi. She explained to her husband that more people drown in bathtubs than in the ocean or swimming pools—that's why he found her with a lifeguard in her bathtub.

The *Marvin* v. *Marvin* case has brought out a new breed of bachelors. "A bachelor," says Burt Reynolds, "has no one to share his troubles. But then, why should a bachelor have troubles?" . . . Milton Berle says, "Bachelors know more about women then married men. If they didn't, they'd be married too."

This bachelor bragged: "I could have married any girl I pleased, but I never pleased any . . ." He could never find a girl that pleased his mother. Finally, he found a girl just like his mom: "She cooked, talked, dressed, and looked like my mom. Mother loved her—but my father hated her."

Another bachelor bragged that he was born with a silver spoon in his mouth. If he was, you can bet there were somebody else's initials on it . . . He was not a bachelor from choice. He asked one girl to marry him for the 15th time after she refused 14 times before. Finally, she said, "Okay, I'll marry you. Anything to keep you from hanging around."

I saw this ad in the paper: "Young man about to be married— seeks acquaintance of older experienced man to talk him out of it."

The Lee Marvin case proves one thing. If you're going to have an affair, make sure you have a good caterer. The way I see it Lee and Michelle had what is commonly known as a trial marriage—now Michelle is asking for bail money.

The Marvin case was a first for Hollywood. Jay Leno went out with a girl last week, they had a bite to eat, went to a movie, had a cup of coffee, and he took her home—an average date. Yesterday, her lawyer called. She's suing him for $11 million—claims he wasted a day of her life.

There's a new game in Hollywood called sex roulette. You have your choice of six girls and one of them is writing a book and will sue.

Did you hear about the resourceful Hollywood starlet who quit her live-in lover because she found a better-paying position?

I know a New York girl who had a beautiful apartment: "I was so happy with my apartment," she told me, "until my louse expired."

"I can't marry you," said the justice of the peace. "This girl is only 17 and you'll have to get her father's consent." The groom-to-be yelled, "Consent? Who do you think the old guy with the rifle is—Daniel Boone?"

This guy goes into the barber shop and says, "How's it going?" The barber says, "Busy." He comes in the next day, "How's it going?" . . . "Busy." Comes in again the third day, says, "How's it going?" The barber says, "Busy." So now the barber says to a friend of his, "There's something going on; next time follow him and see where he goes." Next day, here he comes, "How's it going?" . . . "Busy." The friend follows him, comes back and the barber says, "Where was he going?" . . . The guy says, "Your house."

The young attractive housewife was a bit surprised when her husband's best friend dropped by one afternoon and offered $500 to make love to her. Thinking the extra money would come in handy, she took it and fulfilled her part of the bargain. Later that afternoon, the husband came home and asked, "Did David stop by today?" "Yes, he did," she stammered. "Why do you ask?" "Well, he told me he was coming by to return the $500 I lent him last week."

The *Post* biography of itchy Margaret Trudeau tells about her walking out on her Prime Minister to lead a wild life. If she did all the things the gossips say about her, she could wind up in a bottle on a shelf in Harvard.

This politician came home and found his wife making love to his best friend. "Max," he said to his pal, "*I* must—but *you*?"

My neighbor likes to chase girls. When some gossip told his wife about it she said, "Dogs chase cars, but when they catch them, can they drive?" . . . The wife said to her husband, "I know you're cheating. I know where you're cheating, I know with whom you're cheating—I just don't know *how*!" . . . He burst into his wife's bedroom and shouted, "You miserable cheater—now I know everything!" She said coolly: "Oh?—When was the battle of Bunker Hill?"

A seventyish wife came home to find her husband making love to a neighbor. Furious, she slapped him; he lost his balance and rolled down the stairs. The family doctor phoned her to ask why she hit her husband—the poor guy had suffered a sprained shoulder. "Well, doc," she said, "if he can do what he did at 75—I figured he could fly."

A friend was telling the boys at the Friars: "I've been married for 25 years, but I've never stopped being romantic. Of course, if my wife finds out about it, she'll scream her head off."

Cheating isn't exactly new. You can read about it all through the Bible . . . Coming home very very late one night, Adam found Eve waiting angrily, "Late again," she pouted. "You must be seeing some other woman." "I consider that accusation wildly absurd," shouted the outraged Adam. "You know perfectly well that you and I are quite alone in this world." With this, Adam retired for the night. Something soon caused him to awake with a start. There, hovering over him, was Eve—painstakingly counting his ribs.

Earl Wilson notes, "Living together is such a vogue now, many married couples keep their wedding a secret so they won't appear old-fashioned." I asked Earl, "What do you call a man who's been lucky in love?" He said, "A bachelor."

My neighbor was complaining to her husband: "I'm so embarrassed at the way we live. My father pays our rent, my aunt buys our clothes, my brother sends us food money. I'm sorry we can't do better than that." He said, "You *should* be sorry—you've got two uncles who don't send us a dime."

This old couple had been married for a long time, and she wasn't feeling good, so they went to the doctor. He examined her and said, "You two have been getting together too much. You better stay away from him or you're gonna die; and you better leave her alone, or you're gonna kill her." So they went home and he said, "Well, I reckon I'd better sleep downstairs," and she said, "I reckon so." And he did for a long time. Then one night he couldn't sleep. So he got up and started upstairs and met her coming down. He said, "Where're you going?" She says, "I'm just coming downstairs to die." He said, "That's funny, I was just coming upstairs to kill you."

The most trusting husband I know is the one who thinks his wife spent the night in church because she came home with a Gideon Bible in her hand.

Two neighbors were discussing an incident on their block. "It was terrible. Joe found his wife with Charlie. He knocked him unconscious, pulled all his teeth out with a pair of pliers, and gave him third-degree burns with a blowtorch." The neighbor said, "It could have been worse" . . . "How could it have been worse?" The other said, "The night before, I was with Joe's wife."

Arriving home unexpectedly from a business trip, the husband found his wife with his best friend in the "begat" position. "Look here," the husband shouted, "just what do you two think you're doing?" The wife said to the man beside her, "See! Didn't I tell you he was stupid?"

I asked my neighbor why he was getting a divorce. He said, "My wife called me an idiot." I said, "But that's not sufficient grounds for divorce." He explained, "Well, it was like this. I came home unexpectedly and found my wife in the arms of her lawyer, so I asked, "What's the meaning of this?" And she said, "Can't you see, you idiot?"

The *Post* got a call from a woman who wanted her husband's name put in the obituary column because she'd found him cheating with his secretary. "How long has your husband been dead?" asked the editor. "He starts tomorrow," she answered.

The Frenchman was on trial for killing his wife for having an affair with a neighbor. When he was asked why he shot the wife instead of the lover, he answered, "Ah, m'sieur, is it not better to shoot a woman once than a different man every week?"

Frank came home unexpectedly and found his wife in the arms of the baker. "I'm ashamed of you!" he shrieked, "Why are you making love to the baker, when it's the butcher we owe money to!"

"How active is your love life?" The salesman said, "Every Monday, Tuesday, Wednesday, and Friday, regularly." The doc said, "Maybe your problem is in that area—I suggest you cut out Fridays." The salesman said, "Gee, I can't do that, Doc, that's the only night of the week I'm home."

The 68-year-old banker married his 22-year-old secretary. After only one month she caught him cheating with a 50-year-old woman. "What has she got that I haven't got?" the young secretary asked. "Patience!" he answered.

The beautiful wife of the Englishman died. At the funeral, although the husband controlled his grief, the wife's romantic and devoted admirer sobbed loudly. The husband put his arm around him and said sympathetically, "Don't be upset, my friend, I'll marry again."

Two ladies met in a department store. "I met your husband," said one. "What a brillant man—I suppose he knows everything." The other said, "Don't be silly—he doesn't suspect a thing."

Nobody even expects marriages to last anymore. In California it's now legal to sign your marriage license in pencil . . . "For some people marriage is like peanuts," says Zsa Zsa. "You can't stop at one."

Maybe I'm old-fashioned, but I'm against the idea of people living together unless they're married or in the army . . . A new study says over 30% of the wives in America have had extramarital affairs. That's not good enough for me—I need names . . .

I'm all for marriage. The only way to find out what a woman really thinks of you is to marry her . . . "Married men are happier than bachelors," says Paul Newman. "There's something calming about knowing the worst . . ." I asked my secretary, "How come you aren't married?" She explained, "I'm looking for the perfect man." I asked if she had found him. She said, "Yes, but he was looking for the perfect woman."

When a friend of Elizabeth Taylor Wilding Hilton Todd Fisher Burton Burton Warner got married recently, she sent a telegram to the happy couple wishing them, "All the happiness I have had on a number of similar occasions."

The husband came home excited and told his wife, "I've found this great job—good salary, free health insurance, paid holidays, and four week vacations." She said, "That's wonderful, darling." He said, "I knew you'd be pleased—you start Monday."

Cheating has become the new status symbol in America: "We can't go on meeting like this, dear," he told his wife. "My secretary is getting suspicious . . ." My secretary told me, "I'm in love with him. He loves me, we both enjoy the same things, he earns plenty of money, we're really happy together. My problem is—what shall I tell my husband?"

The husband wired home that he had been able to wind up his business trip a day early and would be home on Wednesday. When he walked into his apartment, he found his wife with another man. Furious, he picked up his bag and stormed out; he met his mother-in-law on the street, told her what had happened and announced that he was filing suit for divorce in the morning. "Give my daughter a chance to explain before you do anything," the older woman pleaded. Reluctantly, he agreed . . . An hour later, his mother-in-law phoned the husband at his club. "I knew my daughter would have an explanation," she said, a note of triumph in her voice. "She didn't receive your telegram."

My neighbor saw this guy in front of his house, jogging naked. "How come you're jogging without any clothes on?" he asked him. The answer was "because you came home early."

The next door neighbor shouted, "Come with me. Your best friend is in a car down the street making love to your wife." The husband dashed down the street. "You're wrong," he told the neighbor when he came back. "I don't even know the guy."

When the bellhop took the couple to their room, the boy was given a generous tip. "Will there be anything else?" he asked. "No, thanks," said the man. "Anything for your wife, sir?" The man thought for a moment, then said, "Why, yes, come to think of it—bring me a postcard to send her."

First prize at a recent costume ball went to a young woman wearing a maternity jacket over her dress, together with the sign: "I should have danced all night."

"You look troubled," I told my friend. "What's your problem?" He said, "I'm going to be a father." I cried, "That's wonderful!" He said, "What wonderful?—My wife doesn't know it yet."

The traveling man went on the road for his monthly trip but kept delaying his return. Every week he sent his wife a wire saying, "Can't come home, still buying." Every wire was the same, "Can't come home—still buying." This went on for four months, until his wife finally sent him a wire that said, "Better come home—I'm selling what you're buying."

Doctors, Lawyers, Dentists, & Shrinks

I'm sick of people picking on doctors. Let's look at their side for a change. My doctor says, "I'm well aware the cost of medical care is outrageous—but so is the price of yachts . . ." I wish I'd been a doctor. My doctor's a surgeon. Handles four operating tables at once and makes $800 an hour—plus tips.

The doctor in my building is a G.P. That's a general practitioner. That's the kind of doctor you go to when you're not sick. For $25 he'll take your temperature and give you the name of a specialist. . . . He's now into socialized medicine —that's when the doctor takes off all his clothes, too.

Several women were chatting at lunch. One was bragging about her doctor: "He's just marvelous. He's tall and handsome and he takes care of all my aches and pains. He knows exactly what's wrong with me before I tell him and always prescribes the right medicine. You should go to him." One of the ladies said, "But I don't need to go to a doctor—there's nothing the matter with me." The first woman said, "Oh, but my doctor is so wonderful—he'll find something."

My doctor just doesn't know how to deal with people. For example, whenever he loses a patient, he notifies the next of kin by sending them a candygram . . . This loaded dowager consulted the doctor about a face lift. "How much will it cost?" she demanded. He said, "$5,000, madam." She complained, "That's too much—isn't there something cheaper?" He answered, "You might try wearing a veil."

My neighbor was bragging about his doctor: "He's got a great pair of hands—ask any cocktail waitress in town . . ." He said, "My doctor works fast. I could tell he was in a hurry to finish the operation by his instructions to the nurse: "Clamp . . . sutures . . . putter . . ."

My mother was right. I should have been a doctor. They got it made. I know one girl who broke her engagement to a young medic. First she had to return all his presents. And then he sent her a bill for 38 house calls.

Did you hear about Dolly Parton? She came down with a chest cold—the doctor who treated her is recovering nicely.

Remember, an apple a day keeps the doctor away. So does not paying your bills.

Doctors are raising their rates again. They say, "All our costs are going up. Medicines, bandages, green fees, golf cart rentals . . ." My doctor said he broke 80. I thought he was lying until I found out he meant patients . . . My neighbor said he had a very delicate operation—in which the doctor separated him from his life savings.

A doctor is someone who acts like a humanitarian and charges like a TV repairman. . . . Anyone who has paid an obstetrician fee knows that Americans aren't born free—one of the reasons an obstetrician is so busy and successful is because he has so many men working for him.

Medical costs are really getting too high. The other day I wasn't feeling well and my doctor gave me a prescription and said, "Take one pill as often as you can afford it . . ." And one bit of advice: Don't leave the hospital until you're strong enough to face the cashier. . . .

I knew my neighbor's son was serious about going into medicine. Right after he took my pulse—he took my credit rating . . . We all knew he would be a big success as a doctor when he first opened his practice. He had all the right equipment: X-ray, electrocardiograph, cash register . . . But you can't complain about his prices. He is one doctor who still believes in house calls. His idea of a house call is— you call at *his* house.

Doctors should let well enough alone . . . There are so many quacks practicing medicine today, it's just not healthy to get sick . . . This doctor walked through his crowded waiting room and said he was going outside for a minute to double-park his car. "In the meantime," he said to his patients, "Don't anbody get better."

The doctor was telling the patient, "You are going to need an operation and you shouldn't put it off." The man wanted to know how much it would cost. "Counting the hospital bill, about $5,800," he said. The man was distraught. "I don't have that kind of money in cash." The doc said, "Okay. Could you pay $157.50 a month?" The man said, "Yes—I can manage that, but that amount sounds kind of funny. It's just like buying a car." The doc said, "I am."

One doctor I know was asked if he could admit to any mistakes. He said, "Yes, I once cured a millionaire in only three visits . . ." My doctor is very upset because he recently made a mistaken diagnosis. He told the patient he had a common cold and later he learned the guy could have afforded pneumonia . . .

We think we are all born free until the doctor's bill comes in . . . My doctor has just made a major breakthrough. He raised his fee to $75 . . . The doctor visited my neighbor in his hospital room: "We'll have you up and complaining about my bill before you know it," he said in his best bedside manner . . . "Just pay one half of what you offered to pay me when you thought you were dying."

Doctors don't always win every round. My doctor phoned the plumber to repair a clogged-up sink. "Tell you what, doctor," the plumber said, "just put two aspirins in the sink and I'll be along in a few hours to see how you're getting along. . . ." My doctor likes to mix business with pleasure. Last week he was at a cocktail party and his hostess took the opportunity to ask him a few questions about her gall bladder. Two days later she got a bill for $35 for a medical examination. Two days after that, the doctor got a bill for $40 for five martinis and 29 hors d'oeuvres.

Mickey Rooney's doctor was amazed to discover that he had a disease that hadn't been around for about a century. Turned out he caught it from one of the magazines in his waiting room.

The doctor hadn't heard from the man for several years. Now it was 2 o'clock in the morning and his wife had a bad stomachache that he was sure was appendicitis. The doc said, "Relax—it couldn't possibly be appendicitis. She probably has a touch of indigestion—I took out your wife's appendix ten years ago, and in all of medical history I've never heard of anyone having a second appendix." The man said, "That may be true—but haven't you ever heard of anybody having a second wife?"

Show me a doctor who can't remember faces and I'll show you a proctologist.

I'm always a little nervous about going to see a doctor when I realize that doctors are usually described as practicing . . . Medicine has become so specialized these days that if a head cold moves into your chest you have to change doctors . . . I told my doctor I had a ringing in my ear: "What should I do?" He said, "Don't answer it," and then he sent me to a telephone repairman.

When a doctor doesn't know, he calls it a virus; when he does know and can't cure it—he calls it an allergy . . . My neighbor said to his doctor, "I hurt my foot—what should I do?" He said, "Limp" . . . Henny went to his doctor and explained, "I have a trick knee—what should I do?" He said, "Join the circus."

The doctor was trying to encourage a gloomy patient: "You're in no real danger. Why I've had the same complaint myself." The patient said, "But *you* didn't have the same doctor . . ."

The doctor put the stethoscope to Henny's heart. Henny asked, "How do I stand?" The doc said, "That's what puzzles me."

The hypochondriacs are what drive doctors to the golf course. One hypo called her doctor and said, "There is something wrong with my neighbor, she never has the doctor in . . ." The hypo was complaining that "My left arm hurts me, and also my left foot, and also my back and my neck." The doctor muttered something and tapped the patient's knee with a little hammer. "How are you now?" he asked. The patient said, "Now my knee hurts, too."

My doctor is very meticulous—he always washes his hands before he touches my wallet . . . "Doc," I pleaded, "what I need is something to stir me up, give me energy, something to put me in fighting trim. Did you put something like that in this prescription?" He said, "No—you'll find that in the bill."

The doctor asked the sick one if he smoked. The answer was no. He asked, "Do you drink?" . . . "No" . . . "How about keeping late hours?" The answer was no again. The doc said, "How am I going to cure you if you have nothing to give up?"

Did you ever stop to think that two professions that wear masks in this country are holdup men and surgeons? And hospitals aren't exactly cheap. A room now is $100 a day—of course overnight is extra.

Two doctors met at a convention. The first one said, "I know you've been making love to my wife. What do you think of her?" The other said, "Don't you know?" The first said, "Yes, but I wanted a second opinion."

Sign in doctor's office: "Any man who isn't ruptured yet just isn't carrying his share of the load."

"I called my doctor the other day and told him I had taken an overdose of aspirin. I said, "What do I do?" He said, "Take two aspirins and call me in the morning."

My doctor is a genius. He's performed 500 operations and never cut himself once! He invented a new miracle drug that is so powerful, you have to be in perfect health to use it.

The loving wife asked the doctor after a hard day: "Did the operation go okay?" He said, "Yes, dear. I managed to do it in the nick of time—another couple of hours and the patient would have recovered without it."

The insurance company asked the wife, "Did he die a natural death?" She answered, "Oh no, he had a doctor."

Professor Von Drek went to a psychiatrist and insisted he examine him. "What do you do for a living?" the head man asked. "I'm a psychiatrist myself." "Then why don't you examine yourself?" Von Drek answered, "I'm too expensive."

The doc said to the call girl: "You look run down—I suggest you stay out of bed for a week or two."

I don't want to say he's inept but my doctor once diagnosed my illness as a case of walking pneumonia. I said, "What should I do?" He said, "Take taxis."

One doctor I know was called at 5 A.M. by a hysterical lady who just kept screaming into the phone. He finally had to get out of bed, get dressed, and make a house call. He figured if his wife was that upset—he'd better go home!

A doctor diagnosed a patient's run-down condition as being caused by money matters: "Calm yourself," he ordered, "only a couple of weeks ago I had another patient here who was very nervous because he couldn't pay his tailor bills. I told him to forget about them and now he feels great." The patient said sadly, "I know—I was his tailor."

Recent surveys show that on any given day, during office hours, 4 out of 5 doctors would rather be on a golf course.

I really got some doctor—he speed-reads his medical books.

The doctors are in great shape, but my doctor has never violated his oath—the one he took 22 years ago, when he swore to become a millionaire.

My neighbor happens to be a doctor who was an auto worker while studying medicine. He built cars in Detroit. Ever since he became a doctor most of his patients have been called back for repairs.

My doctor saved my life once. I called him to the house and he never showed up.

Morris went to the doctor for his yearly checkup and was greatly relieved when the doctor gave him a clean bill of health. "Just remember one thing, Morris. Your body is your home. So keep it clean and neat." The patient said, "I got ya, doc, I'll call in a woman twice a week."

The best way to get a doctor to make a house call—is to marry him. This doc was awakened at 4 in the morning by a caller who wanted to know how much he charged for a house call. "Twenty-five dollars," the sleepy doc muttered. "And how much is an office visit?" "Fifteen dollars." The caller said, "Okay, doc, I'll meet you at your office in 15 minutes."

I recently bought a used car, but it's almost new. It was formerly owned by a doctor who only used it to make house calls.

My doctor doesn't make house calls—but if you're sick more than five days he sends you a get-well card. He told my neighbor, "You're in excellent shape for a man of 65—forget the fact that you're only 45."

Anyone can find a doctor these days—the caddies all have walkie-talkies.

The guy was complaining that doctors just don't write plainly: "My doctor gave me a prescription and after I had it made up I used it as a complimentary ticket to a show, then as a railroad pass, and now my son plays it on his violin."

Did you hear about the acupuncturist who treats only secretaries—he uses staples.

Tony Vallo says his doctor wears a mask at every operation: "It's not for cleanliness—it's just that in case he makes a mistake the patient won't recognize who did it."

My neighbor is really a hypochondriac—his water bed is filled with chicken soup.

This lady received a bill from her doctor after her son got over the measles. She decided the bill was too high so she called the doctor. "Please remember," the doc said, "that I paid ten visits to your house while your son had the measles and I had many cases at the time." She said, "Well, you please remember that he's the one who infected the whole fifth grade."

Every mother wants her son to become a doctor. I know one actor who decided to follow his mother's advice and became a famous surgeon. One morning he performed a very delicate operation before a group of interns and nurses. When the operation was completed, the audience burst into a spontaneous round of applause—so, for an encore, he took out the patient's appendix.

My neighbor went to see his doctor and complained, "Doc, every bone in my body aches." The doc said calmly, "You should be glad you're not a herring."

This man called the doctor for an appointment. The nurse suggested a date three weeks off. He said, "I may be dead by then." The nurse replied, "You can always cancel the appointment."

The doctor asked his patient: "If I thought an operation was necessary, would you have enough money to pay for it?" The patient asked: "If I didn't have enough money, would you think the operation was necessary?"

Acupuncture is very big now. Don't fight it. When is the last time you saw a sick porcupine? . . . Pat Henry says: "Everybody talks about acupuncture but I can tell you it's not new. As far back as 30 years ago it was big in my Brooklyn neighborhood. Instead of a needle, they used an ice pick—now they call it mugging."

To tell the truth, I tried acupuncture but I don't think I can make it. I called the doctor one night and told him I was in pain. He said, "Okay, take a safety pin and call me in the morning . . ." I have a friend who drowned while taking acupuncture treatments on a water bed.

I ruled out acupuncture when I saw my doctor reading the book *Fun with Needlepoint* . . . It's true that Chinese doctors give you the needle when they treat you—American doctors give you the needle when they bill you.

My doctor won't even give you a checkup until he checks out your checking account . . . I must be honest with you. My doctor only charged me $25 for my X-rays—but he talked me into wallet-size 2 × 4 glossies for $100.

The trouble with ear, nose, and throat doctors is that they ask for an arm and a leg . . . Earl Wilson has come to the conclusion that the only difference between an itch and an allergy is the size of the doctor's bill.

This doctor was perplexed by his latest case. He had given his patient all kinds of tests, but his results were still inconclusive. "I'm not sure what it is," he finally admitted. "You either have a cold or you're pregnant." She said, "I must be pregnant—I don't know anybody who could have given me a cold."

I know one hospital that's so swanky you have to be well before they let you in . . . My neighbor just got out of the hospital. He tells me he got 500 get-well cards from Blue Cross alone . . .

This fellow goes to the hospital for a complete checkup. "Doc," he says, "I'm a mess. My jowls are sagging, I have blotches all over my face, my hair is falling out, and I feel ugly. What is it?" The doctor said, "I don't know what it is— but your eyesight is perfect . . ." He asked for plastic surgery—so they took him to the emergency ward . . .

The patient said to the doctor, "Inflation beat you to the punch—everything you want me to give up for my health, I've already given up because I can't afford it . . ."

The nurse told the doctor, "That Mr. Schwartz who wouldn't respond to treatment, won't respond to his bill . . ." Mr. Schwartz explained, "Doc, I can't pay my bill now—I slowed down like you told me, so I lost my job."

I know hospital costs are out of hand—but I never thought I'd see a self-service operating table.

It's amazing how much a hospital stay can cost. But you get used to it. When the nurse passed my uncle the bedpan, he absentmindedly tossed in a ten-dollar bill and passed it on.

Sign in a hospital in the West: "During this intense weather, and owing to the scarcity of coal, no unnecessary operations will be performed."

The hospital nurse said to the patient: "You're just what the doctor ordered—a patient with a good credit rating."

Lawyers now can advertise just like the butcher, the baker, or the plumber who overcharges . . . My Uncle Charlie, the lawyer, has started advertising his services. He's offering great terms: "$50 down and the rest when you get out of prison!"

An old guy was brought into court on a charge of stealing chickens and was told by the judge that he should have a lawyer. He could pick one out from the many advertised in the paper. "I don't want a lawyer," the poor soul said. The judge asked, "Why not?" He said, "Well, judge, because no matter what happens I want to enjoy those chickens myself."

"If we win this case," said the client, "I'll pay you three thousand dollars." "Okay," agreed the lawyer, "Get some witnesses." The man hunted up several witnesses and won the case . . . "Now that we've won," said the lawyer, "how about my three thousand?" . . . "Okay," agreed the client. "Get some witnesses."

A man bought some merchandise from Irving on the installment plan, but refused to make the last payment. Irving found a lawyer who advertises that for a $50 retainer he can help anybody. Irving gave him the money. The lawyer said, "Thank you. This entitles you to two questions." Irving said, "What! Fifty dollars for two questions! Isn't that very high?" The lawyer said, "Yes, I suppose so—now, what's your second question?"

A former office boy with a large firm was brought to trial by his ex-boss on the charge of stealing $1,000 in postage stamps. He retained a clever young lawyer he found in the yellow pages who made a brilliant defense plea and he was exonerated. "How can I ever repay you?" He told his lawyer. "Just pay my fee, that's all," he replied. "Well," the kid suggested, "I can't pay you in cash, but will you accept stamps?"

It seems the gate broke down between heaven and hell. Saint Peter appeared on the scene and called out to the devil, "Hey, Satan. It's your turn to fix it this time . . . " "Sorry," replied the devil, "my men are too busy to worry about fixing a mere gate . . ." "Well, then," scowled Saint Peter, "I'll have to sue you for breaking our agreement . . ." "Oh yeah," replied the devil. "Where are you going to get a lawyer?"

"Although the evidence is again me," said the old man charged with a crime, "I've got $50,000 in cash to fight the case with . . ." "You'll never go to prison with that kind of money," the lawyer assured him . . . And he didn't. Before he entered prison the lawyer had the $50,000.

If you read something that you can't understand, you can be sure it was drawn up by a lawyer . . . There are two kinds of lawyers: those who know the law and those who know the judge . . . A lawyer is a man who gets two people to strip for a fight, and then runs off with their clothes.

My neighbor's son is taking prelaw in college and it's frightening the way his mind works. He wants his mother and father to break up so he can practice.

"Most women are opposed to divorce," the lady was telling me. "We don't like the idea of sharing our husband's money with a lawyer."

A lawyer and his wife were taking an ocean cruise. The ship hit a storm and the lawyer fell overboard. Almost immediately eight sharks formed a two-lane escort for the guy and helped him all the way back to the ship. "It was a miracle," the lawyer told his wife. "No," said his wife, "just professional courtesy."

Lawyers sometimes tell the truth—they will do anything to win a case . . . Bursting into the lawyer's office, the butcher demanded, "If a dog steals a piece of meat from my shop, is the owner liable?" The lawyer said, "Of course." The butcher said, "Well, your dog took a piece of meat worth $25 about five minutes ago." The lawyer said, "All right—give me another $25 and that will cover my fee."

The prisoner faced the bench. "Tell me," said the judge, "have you anything to offer this court before it passes sentence?" "No, your honor," replied the prisoner. "My lawyer took my last cent."

When a hostile witness preceded each answer with "I think," the lawyer lost his patience and insisted for the third time that the witness tell the court and jury "what you know, and not what you think." Whereupon the witness quietly replied, "I'm not a lawyer; I can't talk without thinking."

I don't know if it's better to tell the truth or hire a lawyer. A good lawyer is a guy who represents you just to make sure you get all that's coming to him.

The attorney reported to his client, "I've finally talked your partner into seeing things your way and he has agreed to a settlement that is very fair to both of you." The client screamed, "Fair to both of us? I could have done that myself —why the hell do you think I hired a lawyer?"

"Judge," the prisoner pleaded, "I just don't know what to do." The judge asked what his problem was. "I swore to tell the truth," he explained, "but every time I try, some lawyer objects."

Do it now. There may be a law against it tomorrow!

My lawyer puts F. Lee Bailey and Roy Cohn to shame. During his last trial, he had the entire jury declared legally insane!

This purse snatcher insisted that he act as his own lawyer. As he cross-examined the victim he asked her, "Did you get a good look at my face when I took your purse?"

I know one lawyer who really worries about his clients. "If they ever get out of jail," he cries, "they will kill me."

The lawyer's wife was complaining about the way their home was furnished: "We need chairs, new lamps, a dining room set." "Listen," he told her, "one of my clients is suing her husband for divorce. He has a lot of money and as soon as I finish breaking up their home—we'll fix ours."

The lawyer asked for a new trial for his client. "On what grounds?" the judge asked. "My client has dug up some money I didn't know he had," the lawyer answered.

A young attorney asked an old one for rules to success as a criminal attorney. "There are two," he answered, "always collect your fee in advance—and always remember that you will not be required to serve the sentence."

The man was in jail for rape, murder, kidnapping, and blackmail. The lawyer said, "I found a loophole in your case. According to Abramowitz versus Adams, January 6, 1911: Book III, page 6, paragraph 13, I think I got the answer. Don't worry, I'll get you out. Just leave it to me. Now I'm leaving for Washington on Monday and I'll be back Friday. Meanwhile—try to escape."

Two lawyers got into a name-calling session before the trial started. "You're a bum—a phony, crooked ambulance chaser," screamed the first one. "And you are a small-time shyster," hollered the other. "Well," said the judge, "now that you've both been identified, I can proclaim this court in session."

I'm tired of listening to people knocking lawyers. I don't disagree—I'm just tired of listening to it . . . After all, if there were no bad people there could be no good lawyers . . . Just remember that honesty is the best policy—because good lawyers come high.

I don't want a lawyer to tell me what I cannot do; I hire him to tell me how to do what I want to do . . . This girl charged that the young man raped her against her will. The young man's lawyer asked, "Isn't it true that you responded to him? Didn't you embrace the defendant also?" She said, "Yes, I did—but it was only in self-defense."

I read a story about some guy that left the bulk of his estate to his lawyers. Say, if everybody did that, a lot of time would be saved . . . "How does it happen you have no lawyer?" the judge asked. The prisoner explained, "Well, I did engage an attorney, but as soon as he found out that I had not stolen the $10,000, he would have nothing to do with my case."

The doctor finally reached his table at dinner after breaking away from a woman who sought his advice on a health problem. "Do you think I should send her a bill?" he asked the lawyer who sat next to him. "Why not," the lawyer said, "you did give her profound advice." The next day, when the doctor went to his office to send the bill to the woman, he found a letter from the lawyer which said, "For legal services —$2000.00."

The accident victim was furious when he got the bill from his lawyer: "Your bill is outrageous," he screamed, "You're taking seven-eights of my damages. I never heard of such extortion." The lawyer answered calmly. "Well, I furnished the skill, the eloquence, and the necessary legal learning for your case." The client said, "Yeah, but I furnished the case itself." The lawyer retorted, "So what? You don't have to have a college education to fall down an elevator shaft."

The man who said "Talk is cheap" never hired a good lawyer.

A head doctor is a man who asks a lot of questions that your wife asks for nothing . . . You go to a shrink when you're slightly cracked, and keep going till you're completely broke. . . . My neighbor told his psychoanalyst that he had an uncontrollable desire to write bad checks and asked him what he should do. The shrink said, "Make sure you pay me in cash."

A psychiatrist is the next man you start talking to after you start talking to yourself . . .

There's a doctor in Beverly Hills who calls himself "The Friendly Psychiatrist." He lies down on the couch with you . . .

A psychiatrist is one who stops you worrying about your problem—and starts you worrying about your bill . . . If talk is cheap, why do those shrinks charge $75 an hour?

The head doctor informed his female patient that she was in good shape: "It's taken a long time, Mrs. Schwartz," he said, "but I think we've finally cured you of the fixation that you're Elizabeth Taylor." The lady said, "That's wonderful!

But just remember to send your statements to Senator John Warner—he pays all the bills."

A shrink is a person who will listen to you as long as you don't make sense . . . The doc asked the patient what dreams he had the night before. "I slept fine," he explained, "I didn't have a dream all night." The doc scolded, "How do you expect me to cure you if you don't do your homework?"

The delicious blonde was telling her doctor the problem: "Whenever I have a drink, I want to make violent love to the first man I see." The psychiatrist said, "Don't worry— as soon as I've mixed this cocktail we can sit down and discuss it."

The doc asked, "Are you troubled by sexual fantasies?" She said, "No—I enjoy them" . . . He said, "Then you should be happy." She said, "What's happy? Sixteen children I've had by that husband of mine and he doesn't even love me. What is there to be happy about?" The doc suggested, "Well, imagine what it could have been like if he did love you?"

These two psychiatrists were talking shop. One remarked, "I have a patient with a split personality." The other sneered, "That's not uncommon." The first shrink said, "That's true, but in this case they both pay."

You go to the shrink because you feel vaguely miserable and hopeless, and within less than an hour and fifty dollars later you know what your problem is. You are not vaguely miserable and hopeless. You are clearly depressed and despondent . . . "Wassa matter with me?" he asked the doc. The shrink said, "You're crazy." The man said, "I want another opinion." The doc said, "Okay—you're ugly, too."

A lady visited a psychiatrist for the first time. He invited her into his office and asked her to make herself comfortable on the couch. Seeing that she was hesitating and seemed to be shy, he said, "Just lie back and get comfortable. This is the way I have all of my patients talk to me. This is an important part of your treatment . . ." The woman did as she was told. She reclined and began to relax . . . "Now," the doctor said, "Let's begin at the beginning. How did your troubles begin?" . . . "Exactly like this," she said.

A patient was brought to a psychiatrist by friends, who informed the doctor that the man was suffering from delusions that a huge fortune was awaiting him. He was expecting two letters which would give him details involving the deed to a rubber plantation in Sumatra and the titles to some mines in South America . . . "It was a difficult case and I worked hard on it," the pyschiatrist told some colleagues. "And just when I had the man cured—the two letters arrived!"

Every comic has a favorite psychiatrist story. Henny Youngman: "The man comes to a head doctor and says, 'Doc, nobody talks to me.' The doc says, 'Next'" . . . Milton Berle: "Man goes to a psychiatrist. The doc says, 'What do you do?' The man says, 'I'm an auto mechanic.' The doc says, 'Get *under the couch'*" . . .

Bob Hope tells about a caterpillar that met a friend at her psychiatrist's office: "Are you coming or going?" . . . "If I knew that I wouldn't be here."

The young shrink asked the veteran: "My first question is, what is it that wears a skirt and from whose lips comes pleasure?" . . . "A Scot blowing bagpipes," the veteran answered . . . "Right," said the younger one . . . "Now, what is it that has smooth curves and at unexpected moments becomes uncontrollable?" . . . "A good man's bowling" . . . "Right! What do you think of when two arms slip around your shoulder?" . . . "Why, a rugby tackle," replied the veteran . . . "Right said the young doctor. "All your answers were amazingly correct. But you'd be surprised at the silly answers I keep getting!"

An actress friend phoned me and cried, "I've just heard my husband wants a divorce." I said, "So what? You're beautiful and talented, you'll find another man." She said, "I know, but my psychiatrist is out of town and I just don't know what to think."

A recent survey shows that 3 out of every 5 Americans are seeing psychiatrists—the other 2 are psychiatrists. Sam Levenson says his first visit to an analyst was a big letdown. "I was paying him $50 for a ten-minute visit and all he did was ask me the same questions my father used to ask: 'Who do you think you are anyway?'"

Woody Allen: "I went to a psychoanalyst for years and it helped—now I get rejected by a much better class of girls . . . Henny Youngman had a nightmare. He dreamt that his mother was Dolly Parton and he was a bottle baby.

The psychiatrist asked his patient, "Why are you taking your troubles to bed with you?" He said, "What else can I do? My wife refuses to sleep alone."

"I've got a problem," one patient said. "I live in a lavish home with a pool, servants, four cars, a cabin cruiser, a new plane . . ." The doc said, "So what's your problem?" He said, "That's my problem. You see, even with commissions, I never make more than $175 a week."

"Mrs. Schwartz," said the doctor, "your husband must have absolute rest." "Well, doctor," the woman remarked, "he won't listen to me." Hm," nodded the doctor, "a very good beginning, a very good beginning."

A beautiful girl walked into the psychiatrist's office and he immediately leaped at her, kissing her, grabbing her, and making passionate love to her. When he pulled away he said, "Okay, that takes care of my problem—now what's on your mind?"

If you wonder why a psychiatrist is called a shrink, after a few visits just look at your bank account.

The lady told her psychiatrist that she had been married for 12 years and had 11 children. She asked, "Do you think I ought to write a book?" He said, "No—I think you ought to read one."

The guy complained to the psychiatrist that his wife was really weird. "She talks to her plants." The doc said, "So what, a lot of people talk to their plants." He said,"By telephone?"

Two psychiatrists met. One was rumpled, worn out, exhausted, and depressed. The other, happy and elated, said, "I had a great day—busiest in years." "So how could you be so fresh and cheerful after listening all day to troubles and complaints?" "Who listens?"

When you go to a psychiatrist you are sure of one thing—*he* is getting cured.

My psychiatrist told me to speak freely—then he charged me $100 . . . Come to think of it, it's pretty silly to pay a therapist to tell you what's wrong with your personality. Your friends would be glad to do it for free.

Before psychoanalysis, everything a child did was the child's fault. Now everything a child does is his parents' fault . . . One mother noticed her little boy was drawing everything in heavy black crayon. He drew black horses, black cars, black barns. Disturbed about what was going on in his mind, she called a psychiatrist who finally got at the root of the trouble—it was the only crayon he had.

Dreams are required homework for all patients: "I had an awful dream," he told the doctor. "I was on a desert island, and there were three beautiful girls with me and no one else." The shrink asked, "And you call that an awful dream?" He said, "Oh, I forgot to mention, in my dream I was a girl, too."

"I went to see a psychiatrist. He said: "Tell me everything." I did, and now he's doing my act . . .

Mom took her little boy to a head doctor and asked, "Can a 10-year-old boy marry a beautiful star like Raquel Welch?" The doc said, "Of course not—it's ridiculous." The mother said to the kid, "See, what did I tell you? Now go and get a divorce!"

The movie star went to see her psychiatrist and asked, "Do you think I ought to have my nose fixed, you know what I mean?" The doc said, "No, Barbra, if you do you'll be just another pretty face from Brooklyn."

The guy went to a psychiatrist and complained: "My wife and I bought a water bed and lately I find she's drifting away."

You can't win 'em all. The other day this man paid a psychiatrist $100 to be cured of an inferiority complex and the next day he was fined $25 and costs for talking back to a traffic cop.

The head man tried to tell his patient that she was depending too much on pills. "You've got to stop taking those pills—they're habit-forming." She said indignantly, "Now that's ridiculous. How could they be habit-forming—I've been taking them every day for 25 years."

A psychiatrist is a guy who when a beautiful hunk of woman enters a room—watches everybody else.

Two men were arguing at their club. One shouted at the other, "My psychiatrist can beat your psychiatrist any day." And the other yelled back, "Yeah?—Well my psychiatrist can cure your psychiatrist."

"My analyst says I have a persecution complex," my neighbor's wife said, "but he's just saying that because he hates me."

The psychiatrist warned his new nurse: "Please remember when you answer the phone to say, 'We're very busy' and not 'It's a madhouse.'"

Danny Marvin's psychiatrist is under contract to a large chain of Chinese restaurants. You lie on a couch, and he explains your fortune.

My neighbor was having trouble with his wife. The psychiatrist suggested, "Treat your wife nicely, gently, like a guest." He went home and treated her like a guest—and she checked out.

This guy awoke one morning and discovered lilies growing right out of the top of his head. He ran to his psychiatrist to show him. The doc said, "This is fantastic—now where on earth do you suppose these flowers came from?" The guy yelled, "Look at the card! See who sent them!"

I just paid my dentist bill, now there's a cavity in my wallet . . . I went to the dentist and found my wisdom tooth is retarded.

My dentist gave me a thorough examination. He examined my bank account carefully . . . I asked him what my entire job was going to cost. He said, "I'll put it to you simply—just put your money where your mouth is . . ."

My dentist is cheap—mainly because he doesn't have a lot of fancy equipment . . . like a sink. When he's finished working on you, he says, "O.K., rinse and swallow!" . . . I was sitting in the chair when my dentist stuffed cotton in his ears. I asked if the sound of the drilling was that hard to take and he said, "No but the sound of the screaming is!"

Joan Rivers says she goes to a dentist who charges only five dollars a cavity: "I give him five dollars and he gives me a cavity" . . . The doctor told Gilda Radner she had a mouth full of cavities. He asked, "Shall I fill them with gold or silver?" She screamed, "Gold or silver? I can't even afford to fill them with meat."

Phyllis Diller asks, "Have you tried to make an appointment with a dentist lately? They want you to plan your toothache six months in advance." Phyllis says, "I just got my dentist's bill—I think he's pulling my leg, too . . ."

A survey shows that whiskey drinkers get more cavities than milk drinkers—but they go to the dentist in a much better frame of mind . . . Like the tough old farmer who staggered into the dentist's office with a master toothache but couldn't get up the courage to have the molar extracted. The dentist poured him half a dozen shots of whiskey and begged, "Now step in the chair." The farmer growled, "I'd like to see the bum who'd dare touch my teeth now."

Sign in my dentist's office: "Get your 1981 plates here."

I wish I had a dental appointment to cancel—it always brightens my day.

Nothing prompts the payment of an old dental bill like a new toothache. Be true to your teeth and they won't be false to you.

"I'm sorry," the dentist said, "but you cannot have an appointment with me this afternoon. I have 18 cavities to fill," and the picked up his golf bag and went out.

My dentist is painless—he doesn't feel a thing. A real painless dentist is one who forgets to bill you.

The little old lady had some false teeth made. A week later she returned to the dentist to complain that they didn't fit. The doctor gave her a bite test and said, "These seem to fit fine." She said, "I'm not talking about my mouth—they don't fit in the glass."

The patient was nervous and asked the nurse if the dentist was painless as advertised or "Does he operate and drill for the kick of it?" The nurse said, "Not this doctor. He never operates unless it's absolutely necessary. In fact, if he doesn't need the money, he won't lay a hand on you."

Dentists are the modern Robin Hoods. They take from the rich and the poor alike—and keep it . . . With the dollar being obsolete, my dentist says this is a great time to invest in gold fillings. In other words, put your money where your mouth is . . . I don't want to say my dentist charges too much, but last week he put in a gold crown—I think it belonged to Queen Elizabeth.

Dentists are now outdoing doctors with the fee-splitting bit. They send you to orthodontists, root canal specialists, gum mavens, etc. Bob Hope says, "All my dentist does is make appointments for me to see other dentists. I'm not sure if he's really a dentist or a booking agent."

Dentists scare me to death. On my last trip to the dentist, I yelled and screamed and begged for novocaine. And that was in the waiting room! . . . A mother grew enraged when a dentist charged her $80 for pulling her small son's tooth. "I thought you only charged $15 for a tooth-pulling," she told him. The dentist replied, "That's right. But your boy screamed and cried so loudly that he frightened four new patients out of my waiting room."

The poor soul was having trouble and asked the dentist what he charged for extracting a tooth. "Fifty dollars," he was told. "Fifty dollars for only two seconds work?" The dentist said, "Well, if you wish I can extract it very slowly."

The dentist told his patient: "I've got good news and bad news. Which do you want to hear first?" He said, "Give me the bad news." The doc said, "You have six teeth that must come out, you need a lot of root canal work, your gums are all diseased." "The patient asked, "What's the good news?" The dentist said, "I broke 80 on the golf course yesterday."

Show Business

There's no business like show business. Stanley Siegel told me, "I just hired a high-priced press agent to increase my recognition among the public. He says that when he's through my name and face will be seen constantly by everyone in America. He's very exclusive. I'm his fourth client—his other three were Judge Crater, Amelia Earhart, and Walter Mondale."

Fame is a wonderful thing, maintains composer-director Abe Burrows. "When I was a nobody in my hometown," he told me, "they used to yell, 'There goes that bum!' Now that my name is nationally known, they sure have changed their tune. Now they yell, 'There goes that bum Abe Burrows!"

The agent was convincing the producer: "Man, have I got a sensation—built like Muhammad Ali, sings like Tom Jones, and acts like Richard Burton." The producer said, "Wonderful. Bring him in." The agent said, "Trouble is—it's a girl."

The fans keep writing. One sent a loving note to Johnny Carson: "I never miss your show—I never see it, so I never miss it . . ." Burt Reynolds got a special delivery from a lady in Boston: "Dear Burt: Please marry me and I'll never bother you again . . ."

The obsequious fan kept interrupting Dean Martin's drinking. For the first ten minutes he was only a pest; after that be became annoying. Finally he said, "I think you're the greatest. What else can I say?" Dean suggested, "You can say good-bye."

"Sam," said the agent, "I want you should meet Bubbles La Verne, a sensational new stripper I have just discovered. She will be a knockout as the feature in your club . . ." Sam looked the shapely cutie up and down, removed the cigar from his mouth and said: "Well, don't just stand there, sweetheart. Undo something."

The producer ran home from the set for lunch one day and found an actor in bed with his wife. "What the hell are you doing?" The actor said, "Well, I just finished a small part in *Mash*, I'm auditioning for David Merrick, and I'm going to play a doctor on a soap opera."

The famous actor entertained many young ladies in his dressing room. After one matinee, the idol handed the girl a pass for his performance that night. "But," she pleaded, "I'm hungry, I need bread." He emoted, "If you want bread, make love to a baker. I'm an actor—I give passes."

The great John Barrymore lectured on Shakespeare at one girl's college. After, one girl asked, "Considering the extreme youth of Romeo and Juliet, do you think it possible that they had any actual physical relationship?" Barrymore said, "They certainly did in the Chicago company."

My all-time favorite squelch is the one about the famous Shakespearean actor who is accosted by a bum pleading for a quarter. "Young man," emoted the actor in his best Bard manner, "'Neither a borrower nor a lender be'—William Shakespeare." The bum looked at him and answered, "Screw you—Tennessee Williams."

It was that veteran thespian, George Burns, who said, "I don't think acting is very hard. The most important thing is to be able to laugh and cry. If I have to cry, I think of my sex life—If I have to laugh, I think of my sex life."

One producer suggested we do Shakespeare in the nude: "It's easier to find beautiful new bodies than beautiful new scripts" . . . I saw one movie that was so dirty even the couples in the drive-in theater were watching it . . . That's all changing. One enterprising producer is doing a show next season where everybody on stage will be fully clothed —and the audience will be nude.

Sir Laurence Olivier was asked by a reporter if he still found acting as much fun as it used to be. "Look, son," said Sir Laurence, "I'm 72 years old—nothing is as much fun as it used to be."

This is the season when the Friars roast humans. This month the Friars have cooked such hams as George Jessel, Johnny Carson, Milton Berle, and Robert Merrill and they came out well done. The idea is, "If you can't think of anything nice to say about the guy—let's hear it."

Milton Berle about Don Rickles: "Don is the only man I know who has a film of the attack of Pearl Harbor with a laugh track." Don answered lovingly: "Milton Berle is a household word—garbage is also a household word . . ." Berle returned: "What can you say about Rickles that hasn't been said about hemorrhoids . . ." Don said: "Milton lost his TV show. He knew he was in trouble when he found that 50% of the studio audience wasn't listening."

The Jessel dinner at the Friars brought out the heavy artillery. As the Roastmaster, I was the first to burn: "Jessel has been speaking at dinners since the beginning of time. If you take a closeup of the last supper—he's third from the right . . ." Berle said, "Jessel has more medals than Eisenhower. Actually, the only thing he ever attacked was Sophie Tucker in her dressing room at Loew's State."

Bob Hope said, "George is the only comedian in *Who's Who* and Masters and Johnson . . ." William B. Williams said, "He's still chasing girls—if it's downhill . . ." "If he catches them he forgets what for" . . . Jan Peerce said, "What's with this talk about romance—his idea of an exciting night is to go home and watch his foot fall asleep."

At the Friars roast of the opera star I started: "We have 2 disappointments tonight—Jan Peerce couldn't make it and Robert Merrill could . . ." George Jessel, who showed up without his older brother Isaiah, noted, "Bob went to entertain in the Middle East—he was so popular they were shooting at him from both sides . . ." Berle said, "Merrill needed acupuncture, and he was afraid—so for practice, he made love to a porcupine . . ."

When the Friars roasted Frank Sinatra, Don Rickles remarked, "Hey Frank, if only your zipper could talk . . ." Howard Cosell purred, "Sinatra is an antique relic of yesteryear—he is the Paul Anka of the menopause set . . ." Cary Grant: "On my feet I can't function. To tell the truth, I can't function when I'm lying down either—that's why I love your style, Frank."

Bob Hope loved Johnny Carson: "I think the world of you—and you know what I think of the world . . ." For years the Friars have always roasted the ones they love—tonight we break that tradition in honoring Johnny Carson . . ." "Success hasn't spoiled him—he's still the same arrogant bum he always was."

Hollywood keeps changing. First they had the silents, then the talkies, now the dirties. They are now doing on the screen what they used to do off the screen to get on the screen . . . The rash of nudity in the movies is now reaching epidermic proportions . . . In Hollywood they figure that if all the four-letter words were placed end to end, they'd have a hit screenplay.

Sex is not vulgar—but the pictures *are* . . . In addition to movie ratings like P.G., parental guidance recommended, R, and X we add XXX—not recommended for child, teenagers, man, or beast . . . The language alone would have closed a poolroom in the old days . . . On one marquee they advertized: "On our large screen: sex, lust, passion, and wild love—special student price $1.00."

I went to one X-rated movie last night. Just as a reporter, you understand. I never saw such passion! What excitement! What nudity!—and that was just in the balcony . . . The show as so sexy that in order to keep the audience under control, the theater management had to put saltpeter in the popcorn . . . Actually, it was rated XR: no one admitted without a note from Masters and Johnson!

Dolly Parton says she is thinking of doing another movie. Of course she'll have to have a stunt woman fill in whenever the script calls for her to stand up . . . Now that Dolly was voted entertainer of the year, what will they ask her to impress in the cement in front of Grauman's Chinese Theatre? I read where Dolly had her chest insured for $1,000,000— and that's just against theft.

Hollywood isn't any different now than when Ronald Reagan was in pictures. Reagan still has so many of his pictures on the *Late Show* that he keeps more people up than Mexican food . . .

One producer said about his Hollywood wife: "There's one thing about my wife; she's ten years ahead of her time." I asked, "How do you figure that out?" He said, "Easy, she's already spent my salary for 1991."

The future Hollywood starlet was telling her roommate about her interview with the producer. "How will you act if he makes a pass at you?" she asked. "In all his future pictures," she answered.

I love show people. "There's one nice thing about being an actor," Earl Wilson says. "He doesn't go around talking about other people . . ." Bob Hope received a plaque from the Friars. "I don't really deserve this honor," he said modestly, "but on the other hand I 've got arthritis and I don't deserve that either." Alfred Hitchcock: "I never said actors are like cattle—I said they should be treated like cattle."

Actors have to be tough to take some of those critics. As one actor put it: "Critics don't have ulcers—they give them . . ."

"A critic is a man who knows the way but can't drive the car," says one performer . . . If a critic's work were done by a woman it could be called nagging . . . One first-knifer said about one show: "The cast was well-balanced—they were all lousy . . ." Another killer noted: "The play had a happy ending—everybody was glad it was over."

If criticism had any real power to harm, the skunk would be extinct by now—but the critics keep trying: "The curtain rose at 8:30—and the audience at 8:35," said one critic . . . When Bruce Forsythe, the English comic opened in a one-man show here recently, one critic stabbed, "There were too many in the cast . . ." The critic of a London paper, reviewing a play entitled, *Dreadful Night* wrote just one word: "Exactly . . ." Groucho Marx reviewed one performance: "I saw the show at a disadvantage—the curtain was up."

One producer told Harvey Sabinson of the League of New York Theatres: "I think I got a big hit—I met three of the critics and they each told me that if I change one of the acts I'll have a hit." Harvey said, "That's just great." The producer said, "Yeah, but each picked a different act."

Everything is happening on our stages today—every kind of sex, nudity, violence. One way-out actor-writer went to see an off-Broadway producer and said he wanted to top them all: "I'll go on stage and in full view of the audience, I'll commit suicide." The producer said, "Marvelous—but what will you do for an encore?"

There was an old actor in Hollywood who couldn't find work so he took a job at the zoo where he put on a gorilla costume and climbed into the cage. Ten minutes later, another gorilla was shoved in with him. The old guy yelled, "Help, let me out of here," and the other gorilla said, "Shut up. Do you think you're the only actor out of work?"

Bob Hope told me, "Sometimes I've appeared in theaters after rock groups worked there. You should see those dressing rooms—one whiff and you can play the drums."

I think Milton Berle is the greatest. That's not only my opinion, it's his, too. Once I boldly told him I love him, but the other comics considered him conceited. He shouted, "Me conceited? The Great Berle?"

Comedian Robin Williams's wife was very excited; she told everybody that she was going to have a baby. Barry Gray warned her, "I hope you have a better delivery than your husband."

I love every kind of show business—even the ballet. Although there are some things I don't understand. Why do they have to dance on their toes? Why don't they just get taller girls? I think they would all dance better if they took the shoe trees out . . . Woody Allen admits he doesn't dig the ballet: "The last time I went with friends, there was a lot of money bet on the swan to live."

Now the circus is a different thing. I love circus people. Like the acrobat who married the tattooed woman because "If I get up in the middle of the night and I can't sleep, I can sit up and look at the pictures."

I admit that I go to the opera whether I need the sleep or not. One extra who carries a spear at the Metropolitan Opera complains the job's boring: "Just standing there—I could fall asleep. I would, too—except the guy behind me is also carrying a spear."

The fans can be rougher than the critics. One fan was so excited at seeing all the stars at the premiere that he kept shaking hands with everybody. "You already said good-bye to me twice," I reminded him. He said, "It's always a pleasure to say good-bye to you."

Movies are really expensive to make today. Joe Levine made a picture for a mere $25 million. He posted signs in front of the theater: "Nobody will be seated during the first five million."

Joe says it's one of the most expensive pictures he ever made. It cost one million just for the intermission.

Naturally, Texans aren't too impressed with the movie moguls. As one Texan noted: "$5 million for a picture? I spend more than that on home movies."

One studio head was brought a script of the *New Testament* starting with Matthew, Mark, Luke, and John. "You can't do it for less than 50 million," he was told. "But it will be the greatest spectacle of all time," the mogul said. "Okay—I'll go to 60 million—but it must be with the original cast."

One Hollywood producer was so impressed with the money made by *The Ten Commandments* that he hired a crew of writers to come up with 10 more.

Hollywood is great. Where else can you buy a pocket calculator with unlisted numbers . . . One famous Hollywood writer had a pen name, an unlisted phone, a cable address, and a Swiss bank account. When he died they couldn't find him to bury him.

Beverly Hills is very nice. I was there recently. It was the first time I ever saw a Salvation Army band with a string section . . . And so exclusive . . . It's the only spot in the world where Kentucky Fried Chicken has an unlisted number.

All the new movies are for adults only. If you aren't an adult when you go in, you sure are when you come out . . . I saw one nude picture that was so sexy cops were standing in line to raid it . . . I saw a wild sexy movie from Denmark. It was different. They spoke English, but the sex was dubbed in.

Speaking of movies, I called our neighborhood nudie theater last night to find out what was playing. But all I could hear on the phone was heavy breathing.

To show you how things are speeding up in Hollywood, I just heard of a film star who's starting divorce proceedings three weeks *before* the wedding.

These days almost every actress and actor has half a mind to write a book and lately they've been doing it . . . One actress explained why she became a writer: "It's the only respectable profession where a woman can do her work in bed."

One actor told me that it took him ten years to discover that he had absolutely no talent for writing. I asked, "So you gave up?" He said, "Oh no, by that time I was too famous."

At one party a critic who had read the actress' revealing story of all her love affairs, sex partners, and cheating friends and husbands said to the star, "Enjoy yourself while you can, my dear. After all, you only live nine times."

Bob Hope wanted to write a book of his memoirs. He told me, "I once saw an ad in some Village paper offering to show me how to make a fortune as a writer. It was a picture of a man who looked like a Presbyterian minster and he was pointing right at me saying, 'How do you know you can't write?' So I sent him all my stories, anecdotes, gags, and manuscripts. Three months later I received a reply, 'Now you know you can't write.'"

This woman was looking over all the new books in the library. "Oh dear!" she exclaimed, "just when you think sex has finally been explained, out comes another one."

Lee Marvin's book will be called, "Living together can be hazardous to your wealth" . . . One actress revealed in her book, "My husband bought a water bed for us—I call it the dead sea . . ."

The only thing an actor fears more than losing his mind—is regaining it.

The actor had a miracle drug long before miracle drugs were heard of—he called it flattery. I love actors for their belief in God and themselves—and I hope they forgive me for giving God top billing.

"I'm not conceited," the actor told his agent, "but God knows I have every reason to be." The agent said, "How could you stand up in court and say you're the greatest living actor of all time?" The ham pulled himself up to his full five-feet-two: "I was under oath—I didn't want to commit perjury."

Actors aren't people. Though there are plenty of people who are actors. This ham pleaded with his psychiatrist, "Please, doc, I'm developing a terrible inferiority complex—I'm beginning to think there are other people as good as me."

To most Hollywood writers sex is a novel idea.

Here's a rare one: A Hollywood couple got divorced. Then they got remarried—the divorce didn't work out.

I saw a guy driving a domestic car in Hollywood. The crowd gathered around and hollered, "Yankee go home."

Then there is the bandleader who spent all week on a new arrangement and then discovered that his wife wasn't going out of town after all.

The Hollywood agent tried to sell his new girlie act to the nightclub owner. He raved about her figure which was an unbelievable 72-26-40. The owner wanted to know what kind of dance she did. "Well, actually she doesn't dance at all—she just crawls out onto the stage and tries to stand up."

The roughest guys in Hollywood are the producers. I know one who nobody likes. He took his wife to the tunnel of love and she told him to wait outside.

He says he's given a lot of himself to others—but what he's got left is pretty shabby.

The TV networks are in a ratings war at the moment. They'll do anything except improve their shows . . . My neighbor says: "I'd stop watching TV altogether, if I could remember what it is I used to do . . ." TV is getting to be murder. You turn on the set and you see the worst kind of violence, crime, degeneracy, murder, and rape—and that's only the news.

If you think TV is bad now you should go to the movies and see what it's going to be like 10 years from now . . . The thing that's wrong with TV is that it goes in for movies that are not worth going out to see . . . I love movies on TV, but the trouble is they are cut so much for commercials that one of these days we are going to see *The Five Commandments*.

There's so much sex on television this year that stores won't sell *TV Guide* to anyone under 17 not accompanied by a parent.

Show me a man who laughs when things go wrong and I'll show you a television repairman . . . I'm now putting a kid through college—he's the son of our TV repairman . . . The television in my building is so bad, you can't even eat a TV dinner.

TV is remarkable. The same set that puts you to sleep keeps the neighbors awake . . . I finally figured out why Hollywood makes so many lousy movies—so they can sell them to TV . . . Early to bed and early to rise is a sign that you're fed up with television.

One thing you must admit. Television is educational. My nephew learned three ways to mug a woman, four ways to avoid leaving fingerprints, and five ways to ambush a cop.

The evil that men do lives after them—especially when they're television reruns . . . One TV star's summer replacement didn't work out—his wife found out about her.

When I was a kid you could see two pictures for a dime in any theater. Now it costs you $500 for a TV set and what do you get? The same two pictures.

TV has made dull conversationalists of us all—it even has people to talk about the weather for us.

Television is getting a little too violent for me. The other night this one program had seven murders, three robberies, and one attempted rape—and that was on sermonette . . .

Nobody writes fairy tales anymore. You know why? That's because all the fairy tale writers can make more money writing TV commercials.

I'll say one thing about the new TV shows—I'm ready to go back to violence . . . Let's face it, last year's violence got more laughs than this year's comedies . . . TV is so bad I can hardly wait for next year's paid political programs.

A newspaper reporter was writing a feature story about prison life and was interviewing one of the prisoners. "Do you watch much television here?" . . . "Only the daytime shows," the inmate said. "At night we're locked in our cells and don't see any television . . ." "That's too bad," the reporter said, "but I do think it is nice that the warden lets you watch it in the daytime." "What do you mean, nice?" the inmate said, "that's part of the punishment."

All stations now have TV archaeologists. They're the guys who dig up the movies for the late show . . .

The story goes that Johnny Carson went to see his shrink about those terrible dreams: "Every night I dream I'm telling these fabulous jokes that keep the audiences howling for a whole hour without a stop." The psychiatrist said, "I don't see anything so terrifying about that dream." Johnny said, "You don't? A whole hour without a stop?—That means I'm unsponsored."

Personally, I love those commercials on TV. I go during the ads. A minuteman is anybody who can get to the bathroom and back before the announcer notices his absence . . . A good commercial makes you think you've longed all your life for this thing you never heard of before . . . Those TV dinners we've been buying don't look as great as they look on TV—maybe we ought to get a new tube.

110

Pay TV is here to stay—I just got the bill from the repairman . . . What really got me mad was when my TV repairman sent me a card from a resort hotel that even *I* couldn't afford.

Television surely helps you get acquainted with a lot of new people—mostly repairmen.

Lee Strasberg says he has a five-foot screen in his living room—"and I keep it right in front of my set."

The longest word in the English language is the one following the phrase: "And now a word from our sponsor."

One critic praised the TV show with the double name: "They are trying very hard to win an Emmy for bad taste."

Jackie Vernon tells about his Grandma who was approaching the century mark: "We all made plans for a gala celebration. I said, 'How would you like to go for a ride in an airplane on your 100th birthday?' She said, 'I ain't going to ride in no flying machine. I'm just going to sit right here and watch television—like the good Lord intended I should.'"

Gene Baylos told me: "Our TV man had to take our set back to the store for an adjustment—it needed back payments."

There are two types of people in Hollywood. Those who own swimming pools—and those who can't keep their heads above water.

The actor left it in his will that he be cremated and 10% of his ashes thrown in his agent's face.

In Hollywood they call it carving a career because so much knifing is going on there.

Joan Rivers says: "You can always tell a widow in Beverly Hills. She wears a black tennis outfit."

I know a nice Hollywood couple who finally ironed out the divorce settlement—now they can go ahead with the wedding.

There's a group who have an option to buy the Grossinger Hotel in the Catskills . . . but the family will always manage it . . . To the comedians who took their basic training in the mountains, Grossinger's was the Buckingham Palace of the borscht belt . . . Only around Buckingham this type of dialogue you wouldn't hear: "If I live I'll see you Wednesday—if not Thursday . . ." "Where are you living?" "I'm living Friday . . ." "Close the window, it's cold outside" "So if I close the window it'll be warm outside?"

Some of the greatest comic names came out of the borscht belt, including David Kaminsky, Aaron Chwatt, Jerome Levitch, Milton Berlinger, Murray Janofsky, Rabbi Jacob Masler, Leonard Hacker, Sam Levinson, Irwin Kniberg, and Joseph Abramowitz—better known on the marquee as Danny Kaye, Red Buttons, Jerry Lewis, Milton Berle, Jan Murray, Jackie Mason, Buddy Hackett, Sam Levenson, Alan King, and Joseph Abramowitz—that's me. . . Joey Gottlieb became Joey Bishop. Joey says: "My family wanted me to be a rabbi, but how would it sound: 'Rabbi Bishop.'"

Sid Caesar worked as a musician at a hotel in Woodridge for $15 a week. He fell in love with Florence Levy, who happened to be the boss's niece. "I'd never let my niece marry a bum—a musician," he warned. Sid pleaded with him to see his show that night. After the performance, Sid went to see the boss. "You can marry my niece," the boss said, "You're not a musician."

Two visitors from Dublin looked at the kosher sign at Kutsher's Hotel. "What's it mean?" Murphy asked. Kelly explained, "To you it means nothing, to me it means nothing, but to the Jewish people—that's Duncan Hines."

The borscht belt was one big social hall where the young girls came to meet husbands and the husbands came to meet young girls . . . One hotel in South Fallsburgh instituted a novel policy. No more entertainers—they booked only unmarried doctors and lawyers.

The Catskills hotels planned everything. The rooms were so small, when a girl came to visit a guy she *had* to lie down . . . Like my friend Epstein said, "I regret that I have but one wife to send to the country."

There's a sign at the Nevele Hotel in Ellenville: "L.B.J. slept here . . ." The people on the borscht belt answer questions with questions: "How do you feel?"—"How should I feel?" . . . I saw President Johnson after he visited the Catskills and asked, "Did you enjoy?" He answered, "Why not?"

The borscht belt got so big, the Concord Hotel is thinking of air conditioning the forest. They are planning an indoor mountain, and will have tiger hunting under glass.

A Dictionary
of Comics

A comedian is a person who knows a good gag when he steals one. That's why we are starting a comic's dictionary: to blame—I mean credit—the man who stole it (I mean used it first).

Mothers attempting to discover what makes an ordinary, happy, carefree boy become a comedian ask, "Where did he go wrong?" He lives and breathes laughs. He has a joke file where his brain should be. If you look closely, you will see that he has something in him that makes him stand out from other people—you'll see that he's a little nuts . . .

MILTON BERLE became a comedian when his mother gave him a mouthful of marbles. He dropped the marbles out of his mouth one by one—and when they discovered that he lost all his marbles . . .

STEVE MARTIN'S father gave him a rocking chair. He rocked on it day and night until one day it broke—and when they discovered he was off his rocker . . .

JACKIE VERNON says he became a comedian like a playgirl becomes a prostitute. First you do it for your own enjoyment, then for a few friends, and then you figure you might as well get paid for it.

Anyway, quoting politicians makes about as much sense as Dolly Parton wearing a training bra. So I decided to start a comic's dictionary to quote the comedians not in Congress:

NIPSEY RUSSELL: "My neighbor's daughter hollered up to her mom, 'The bill collector is here. Have you got the money—or do you want me to go out and play for a while?'"

BUDDY HACKETT: "All my wife wants from my life is to take out the garbage. When I'm away on a trip she mails me the garbage."

JAN MURRAY: "Happiness is when you're accused of rape at the age of 70."

BILL COSBY: "If at first you *do* succeed—it's probably your father's business."

DOM DELUISE: "Adam may have had his troubles—but he never had to listen to Eve talk about the other men she could have married."

BILL BOGGS: "I'm paying so much insurance to take care of the future—I'm starving to death in the present."

Famous sayings are often credited to the wrong people: I don't care who claims it, it was *DOLLY PARTON* who said: "It's what's up front that counts."

And it wasn't CHURCHILL who said: "never before have so many owed so much to so few . . ." It was the Director of Internal Revenue.

And it wasn't WILL ROGERS but ZSA ZSA who said: "I never met a man I didn't like."

ARTHUR GODFREY lectures: "The modern American drinks Brazilian coffee from an English cup while sitting on Danish furniture after coming home from an Italian movie in his German car. Then he picks up a Japanese ball-point pen to write a letter to his Congressman demanding that something be done about all the gold that's leaving the country."

MIKE DOUGLAS tells about the young couple who had just finished going over their monthly bills and were down to the last two. "Gosh, honey," said the husband, "we're practically broke. I don't know which to pay—the electric company or the doctor . . ." "Oh, the electric company, of course," answered his wife. "After all, the doctor can't shut off your blood."

MERV GRIFFIN: "Three widowed women were sitting around the pool talking about their deceased husbands. One said, 'My husband was an alcoholic but he was charming. The only trouble was, every night at bedtime he'd get stoned and by the time I got to bed he was dead to the world.' The second widow said, 'My husband was a handsome guy, but on our wedding night I found out he was more attracted to my brother than he was to me.' The third widow said, 'My husband was an advertising executive and he was always wrapped up in his craft and bragging about it, like telling me how GREAT it was gonna be!'"

GEORGE BURNS: "It's hard for me to get used to these changing times—I can remember when the air was clean and sex was dirty."

SHELLEY BERMAN: "The guy who invented hookless hangers is the same guy who invented cars with doors that open inward."

HENNY YOUNGMAN: "I got my own talk show—my wife."

DON ADAMS: "I'm sure my wife will live forever. She has nothing but dresses she wouldn't be found dead in."

PAT HENRY: "I'll tell you how ugly she is. Her mother never told her the facts of life because Mother figured she'd never have to use them."

RODNEY DANGERFIELD: "I get no respect. The way my luck is running, if I was a politician—I'd be honest."

BURT BACHARACH: "Only kisses and money could be so full of germs and still be so popular."

PAT COOPER: "Last week I sat in the waiting room of my doctor's office so long I said to hell with it. I decided to go home and die a natural death."

DAVID BRENNER: "Misers aren't fun to live with—but they make wonderful ancestors."

JACK CARTER: "With taxes rising again, businessmen are now blowing their money on wine, women, and Washington."

RED BUTTONS: "Once $50 a week could feed a family of 6—now it couldn't feed a child of 6."

STILLER AND MEARA: "This bum has no friends—he brought a pet parrot home and it told him to get out."

GEORGE CARLIN points out that the value of the dollar is decreasing while the price of bread is going up: "The moral is save bread."

WOODY ALLEN: "My parents didn't want me—they put a live teddy bear in my crib."

JACKIE MASON: "I know a hot-looking broad who went to Hollywood because she wanted to make love under the stars."

BARRY GRAY said: "An executive friend of mine is so dedicated to his work that he keeps his secretary near his bed in case he gets an idea during the night."

VIRGINIA GRAHAM: "The man who can read women like a book—usually likes to read in bed . . ."

SAM LEVENSON, lecturing at a P.T.A. meeting, said that parents should tell their children about sex when they're old enough to understand and before they're old enough to do what they already did.

"Sex is the most fun you can have without laughing," says PHILLIS DILLER.

"A well-balanced sex life is impossible in a canoe," says MEL BROOKS.

"Sex should not be taught in schools, unless the teacher really wants to learn," says MORTY GUNTY. "They always had sex education in public schools, only it used to be called recess."

ROBERT KLEIN: "It's really not the doctors or nurses or hospitals that are the problem. It's the side effects—like bankruptcy."

DAVID BRENNER: "I just figured it out: If a gal is good for nothing—she'll be bad for nothing."

DAVID STEINBERG: "Insanity is grounds for divorce in some states, but grounds for marriage in all; marriage is like a cafeteria—you pick out something good-looking and pay later."

JACKIE VERNON: "I went to see my doctor about my loss of memory—he made me pay in advance."

JACKIE GLEASON: "I only drink to get rid of warts and pimples—not from me but from people I talk to."

RICH LITTLE: was a judge at a pet show and was instructed to look for obedience, friendliness, loyalty, and good grooming. "Forget the pets," Little said. "That's the makings of a great girl friend."

DAVID FRYE: "She was complaining to the doctor that her husband was too old for her and couldn't consummate the marriage. The doctor gave her some pills for her husband and she left promising him that she would let him know how

121

things worked out. A week later, she came back and said, 'Doctor, the pills were fine. For four days in a row, he did it morning and night . . .' 'That certainly was an improvement,' said the doctor. She replied, 'Oh yes! And just yesterday, he did it three times before he died.'"

CARL REINER: "The guy was up all night and looked like a mess. He explained to his pal, 'I haven't been home all night because I'm afraid of my wife. She knew I had $500 in my pocket last night and she knew I was going to play poker, but she thought it was a 10-cent game. Well, I lost every cent—all $500—and I can't face her.' His friend felt sorry for him and lent him the $500 and told him to go home and face his wife. He said, 'Thanks, pal. Can you do me one more favor? Can you let me have another $100?—I'd like to show her I was a winner.'"

CHEVY CHASE: "My doctor told my wife and I that we should enjoy sex every night—now we'll never see each other."

GOLDIE HAWN: "I'm against sex education in schools—what those kids need is a book on how to avoid it."

SAMMY CAHN says his wife is a compulsive cleaner: "I didn't realize it till I came home one night and found her bathing the tropical fish."

PAT PAULSEN: "I'll never forget my first love. She had a strong sense of patriotism. I found her phone number on the wall of a voting booth."

DEAN MARTIN: "I know my capacity for drinking—the only trouble is I get drunk before I reach it."

RED SKELTON: "I believe in living within my income—even if I have to borrow to do it."

BOB NEWHART: "Two retired traveling salesmen were discussing the old days on the road. One said: 'Do you think there's as much sex going on as there used to be?' The other said, 'Sure—but there's a new crowd doing it.'"

ED McMAHON: "At a swank dinner party, a young lady guest suddenly bent over and her bosom popped out of her low-cut evening gown. An observant waiter immediately rushed to her, shielded her with a napkin, and tucked her back in place. The headwaiter saw it and fired him: "This is an elegant restaurant—when that happens, we use a warm spoon instead of fingers."

BETTE MIDLER: "The salesman finally hit on an agreement with his client. Then he called the bookkeeper and asked, 'Miss Simkow, if someone offered you $8,000, less 8%, how much would you take off?' The voice came back loud and strong, 'Everything but my earrings.'"

JOAN RIVERS: "I just found out the chief cause of divorce—marriage."

JERRY LEWIS: "The Englishman asked the Scotsman, 'Hey, Jack! Is anything worn under the kilt?' He answered, 'Certainly not—everything is in perfect working order.'"

DANNY KAYE: "A wealthy old farmer was having a family reunion with his large family and as they all sat down to the table for Sunday dinner, the old man looked around at his six big strapping sons and said: 'I don't see any grandchildren around this table of mine. I want you all to know that I will give $10,000 to the first one of you who presents me with a grandchild. We will now say grace . . .' When he raised his eyes again, he and his wife were the only ones at the table.'"

MEL BROOKS: "Let's enjoy the sex act before Congress repeals it."

PAUL LYNDE: "The doctor told me to stop smoking. The doctor added, 'And since you're quitting—I'll give you five dollars for your gold lighter.'"

CAROL BURNETT: "Women will be wearing the same thing in brassieres this year."

GILDA RADNER does it to herself: "I spent seven hours in a beauty parlor—and that was just for the estimate."

BOB HOPE said about PHYLLIS DILLER's sexploits: "She couldn't lure you out of a burning building . . ." Hope said: "I make sexier looking things out of pipe cleaners."

GEORGE GOBEL: insists that it takes DOLLY PARTON 45 minutes to get her feet wet under the shower.

JOEY FAYE: said, "It's tough to see DOLLY PARTON in pictures—she keeps falling over too much."

HARVEY KORMAN: "The sexual revolution is here and I'm out of ammunition."

LUCILLE BALL: "I have everything I had 20 years ago—only it's all a little bit lower."

DAVID LETTERMAN: "A woman's place is in the home—and she should go there directly from work."

The sound and fuming of MORT SAHL: "The best thing about analysis is that if you don't make it with them they'll refer you to another analyst. They call it rehabilitation—referral—motivation—therapy. We call it fee-splitting."

SHELLEY BERMAN: "I don't like buttermilk. It's not the buttermilk that bothers me—it's the way the glass looks when you're through that makes me sick."

PHIL LEEDS: "It's easier to work nowadays if you work cleaner, better, and cheaper than anybody else."

PROFESSOR IRWIN COREY: "I come from a neighborhood where the only sound you hear is an occasional cry for help. When I was a kid my living room was decorated as a swamp."

CHARLES NELSON REILLY: "Airlines are always bragging about their safety records—'Flying is the safest way to travel'—I don't know how much consideration they gave to walking."

DANNY THOMAS got a letter he couldn't read: "It's either from my 4-year-old grandson or my 40-year-old doctor."

Diet & Exercise

Dieting is a trying time when you stop eating food and start eating calories . . . "What are you supposed to eat?" one impatient patient growled, "Preservatives, food coloring, cholesterol, calories—it's all bad for us. The only way to survive is to starve to death . . ."

Dieting is the period when you can eat as much as you like, but only of the foods you don't like . . . One doctor I know has worked out some very effective diets. One irritable millionaire patient was given one of those diets to follow. He looked it over with an angry eye and then snarled, "Why do you doctors order a man to cut out just the things he likes?" The doc answered, "Because he never eats or drinks the things he *doesn't* like, so it stands to reason it must be the things he *does* like that are disagreeing with him."

My doctor told me that if I give up drinking, smoking, desserts, and chasing women, I could look forward to a long boring life . . . My brother's wife has come up with a very simple device to make him lose weight—it's called a food bill.

My neighbor's wife tells me, "For years I weighed 175 pounds. I was really fat. Today I still weigh 175 pounds, but thanks to women's lib I don't have to diet. I'm just right—I read the men's side of the weight charts."

The lady next door was terribly excited over the success she was having with her new diet. She optimistically projected several months into the future and announced to her husband that she was giving him a 110-pound wife for his birthday. "Oh, great," he answered, "Whose?"

The best way to lose weight isn't nearly as much fun as the worst . . . One doctor prescribed to his patient, "No rich foods, no meats, no drinks—that should save you enough money to pay my bill . . ." My aunt found a doctor who put her on a wild diet. She can only eat the juices of what comes out of her blender. But she fixed him; for one meal alone she drank two pot roasts, four lamb chops, and a chicken.

My doctor has the greatest diet of all: "Eat all you want, chew—but don't swallow."

I've tried every diet known to fat people, from the Scarsdale to the water diet, and I'm thick and tired of it . . . One doctor put me on a very effective diet. Filet mignon three times a day. In the first week I lost $350 dollars . . . There's a new rice diet that always works; you use only one chopstick . . . I quit the onion diet—I lost 10 pounds and 12 friends . . . I got the simplest diet of all—if it tastes good, spit it out.

My neighbor told me, "I've found this wonderful diet doctor. He lets you eat anything you want—as long as you pay your bill . . ."

A guy I know is on a salt-free diet and he's desperate for salt. He rushes into a restaurant and gobbles down a whole shaker of salt. The waitress asks, "How is it?" He says, "It needs pepper."

One of life's little mysteries: how can a two-pound box of candy make you gain five pounds? My doctor is a consumer advocate. He advocates that I consume less . . . The salesman was dining in the restaurant with his latest flame. "If my doctor could see me with this champagne and caviar," he said, "he'd go crazy." She asked, "Why, are you supposed to be on a diet?" He said, "No—I owe him $500."

Sam Levenson never dieted and defended his avoirdupois: "When I was a kid we all overate. The only proof mamma had that she was a good mother was the fact that her children were fat. To my mother, if you didn't bulge, you were skinny. I had 'baby fat' until I was 37 years old."

Walter bumped into his old pal Charlie on the street and nearly passed him without recognizing him. Charlie looked awful. His face was thin and drawn—bags under his eyes, his clothes hung on him. "Have you been sick?" Walter asked. He said, "No—my wife is on a diet."

Johnny Carson swears he has the solution with the drinking man's diet: "You eat anything you want, but you must also drink two quarts of vodka a day. You don't lose weight; you forget you're fat . . ." Dean Martin has a drinking man's diet that he says can't fail: "The first day you have ⅓ oz. of Scotch at hourly intervals. Second day: 1 oz. of Scotch at ½ hour intervals. Third day: 2 oz. of Scotch with no intervals. You may not lose weight, but those will be the three happiest days you will ever spend."

Show me a gal with a beautiful figure, and I'll show you a very hungry gal . . . Virginia Graham is proud of her measurements: "I happen to have an 18-inch waistline—through the center. Furthermore, I have the same measurements as Sophia Loren—her living room is 18 by 25 and so is mine."

Doctors will tell you that if you eat slowly, you will eat less—particularly if you're a member of a large family . . . A giggling fiftyish woman said coyly to her doctor, "Look at me, I've lost all that fat off my stomach since I was here last.

I wonder where it's gone?" The doc said, "Look behind you lady, look behind."

A diet is what you keep putting off while you keep putting on . . . Jimmy Coco just returned from a West Coast spa and told me, "Years ago being on bread and water was punishment. Today at a health farm you pay a fortune for the privilege."

Buddy Hackett told me his wife went on a new acupuncture diet. "She doesn't eat any differently—she loses weight through leakage."

If you want to keep the right curves from settling in the wrong places, you've got two choices: Eat all you want of things you don't like, or keep your mouth and the refrigerator closed.

If you cheat on your diet—you gain in the end . . . Sam Levenson came up with a foolproof diet but you must adhere to two things: "1, eat only bagels, cream cheese, and lox," and "2, you must live in Iran . . ."

"Most people are terrible at counting calories," Earl Wilson warns, "and they all have the figures to prove it" . . . This salesman and his wife arrived in Chicago on a combined business and pleasure trip. He ordered the biggest and most expensive dinner in the hotel. His wife made some fast calculations. "Charlie," she warned, "that adds up to about three thousand calories." He said, "So what? I'll put them on my expense account."

Jackie Gleason was so fat as a kid, he could only play Seek . . . Buddy Hackett told me he was so fat he was born on June 3, 4, and 5 . . . Gleason went to one of those fat farms that really work. The first day alone he was $3,000 lighter . . .

Buddy's doctor told him he must drop bread from his eating habits. "No bread?" Hackett yelled, "Then how am I going to sop up the gravy?" . . . Buddy saw slender Johnny Carson and needled, "You look like there's a famine in California." Johnny answered, "And you look like you caused it."

I saw Mickey Rooney in *Sugar Babies* and told him how good he looked: "You took off a little height." He said, "I'm not as big a fool as I used to be." I said, "Oh? Did you diet?" . . . He told me his doctor recommended a diet of one ounce of orange juice, two drops of milk, and a handful of bread crumbs twice a day." He asked the doctor if he could borrow a postage stamp because he likes to read while he's eating.

The second day of a diet is always easier than the first—by the second day you're off it.

Does your end justify your jeans? If not, you better reach for Sweet 'n' Low . . . When a man looks a woman straight in the eye, she'd better do something about her figure . . .

The woman was told by her doctor that the best way to take off weight was to wear Saran wrap over her body. When her husband came home that night and saw her in the Saran wrap he cried, "Leftovers again!"

I told the doctor I get very tired when I go on a diet. So he gave me pep pills. You know what happened? I ate faster.

The drunk was at the bar scribbling figures on a napkin. The bartender asked what he was doing. "My wife is on a diet," said the souse, "and she told me she's losing four pounds a week. So, if my figures are correct, I'll be rid of her completely in about 18 months."

Isn't it a shame that calories always taste so much better than vitamins? . . . My next door neighbor is so fat she has to wear stretch jewelry . . . They now have a new Weight Watchers spaghetti. It comes in an unopenable can . . . Then there's the new Volkswagen diet. They shove you into one of those little cars and then you've got to starve yourself to get out.

My mother-in-law did something about her weight—she stopped getting on the scale.

It took a lot of willpower—but I finally gave up trying to diet.

Jimmy O'Rourke says: "Before telling anyone you're going on a diet—be sure to weigh your words." Dieting makes some people so cranky they behave like something's eating *them*."

My friend Marvin just invented a new product—Sweet N' Low hair tonic for fatheads.

The toughest part of a diet isn't watching what you eat—it's watching what your friends eat.

Jimmy Joyce's uncle is a real drinking man—if there's a nip in the air he'll find it. When it comes to drinking he has wonderful self-control—he never drinks unless someone else is buying.

It isn't the travel that broadens one—it's all that rich foreign food.

Right now it's become so bad in the Catskill Mountains— they've had to put another notch in the borscht belt.

Henny says his neighbor's wife is on a diet of coconuts and bananas: "She hasn't lost any weight—but can she climb a tree."

She tried everything to lose weight but now she found the formula. She eats nothing but garlic, onions, and limburger cheese. Nobody can get near her—so from a distance she looks thin.

All you weight watchers have nothing to worry about. If saccharin goes off the market, you can always get artificial sweetening by watching Dinah Shore.

The ones that gain the most in all this are the dieticians— they live on the fat of the land.

Eileen Ford says the best way for overweight people to slim down is to take off their clothes and eat in front of a mirror. I tried doing that last week and I really did eat less—because they threw me out of the restaurant.

I have a friend who doesn't diet and never gains an ounce. He eats six meals a day. An average meal consists of two steaks, four pounds of potatoes, three hamburgers, an apple pie, a malted, an ice cream soda, and a hot fudge sundae— and he still weighs the same, 475 pounds.

She was so fat her yearbook picture was continued on the next page. She went horseback riding to lose weight and it must have worked. The horse lost 30 pounds.

She more than kept her girlish figure—she doubled it.

"How's your wife getting along on her diet?" "Great—last night she disappeared completely."

Have you noticed that when you go on a strict diet—the first thing you lose is your temper? Dean Martin went on that drinking man's diet and he says it's great. He lost eight pounds and three weekends!

The two guys were talking at the bar. One asked: "When a person loses 10 pounds, where does it go?" The other said knowingly: "I guess it just evaporates into space." The first one said, "Just think—at this moment there may be 10 pounds of Sophia Loren floating above us."

So eat, drink, and be merry—for tomorrow ye diet.

Exercise definitely does not pay. This guy trained for a whole year to run the 26 miles in the Boston Marathon. But he had to quit after 25 miles. He went home only to find his wife making love to a guy who quit after a mile.

I have only one thing to say about runners. Anyone who says they run ten miles a day with their muscles aching, their hearts pounding, and their lungs on fire, because it makes them feel good—will lie about other things as well.

Jogging has become a national pastime. Now go convince Zsa Zsa Gabor and Elizabeth Taylor Wilding Hilton Todd Fisher Burton Burton Warner . . . Tip to ladies: miniskirts enable a girl to run faster—and if you're in the park, you may have to . . .

Thousands of Americans have bought books on running for a very simple reason—reading is a lot easier than running . . . Me? I'm doing great—I'm up to 20 pages a day . . . I get plenty of exercise—several times a day I jog to the refrigerator . . . "Jogging pays off," my banker told me. "I caught my secretary yesterday."

The doc explained that, "You burn up the same amount of energy making love as you do jogging around the reservoir." I said, "And you want me to waste it jogging?" He said, "Sure—at least after two laps around the reservoir you don't want a cigarette."

I don't understand why everybody thinks jogging is good for your figure. Did you ever take a good look at a camel?—or a horse? . . . It reminds me of the baseball scout who was raving about a new prospect he had found. It turned out to be a horse. In a tryout, he picked up the bat with his teeth and slammed every ball out of the park. Then they gave him a glove and put him on the field, and he caught everything hit to him. On opening day they put him in the lineup, and he slammed the ball into the far reaches of right field, but then just stood there. "Run," the manager screamed. The horse said, "Run? Are you kidding? If I could run, I'd be at the track."

I don't understand what everybody is running around about . . . I need help with my toothbrush . . . If I have to open the window I call the super . . . I get all the exercise I need—at night I toss and turn a lot . . . My doctor said I should get

136

more exercise, so now when I watch football on TV—I yell louder.

My doctor told me jogging could add years to my life, and I think he was right. I feel 10 years older already. . . "Running is healthy," he says, "It's especially good for the legs, the ankles, and the economy." I asked how it helps the economy. He said, "When you run you're helping provide jobs for people who make sneakers, shorts, running pants, liniment, and doctors who treat you for exhaustion . . ."

The doctor told Henny to run 10 miles every day—it was good for his sex life. After two weeks Henny called the doctor who asked, "Are you running 10 miles a day?" he said yes. The doc acked, "So—how's your sex life?" He said, "Who knows? I'm 140 miles from home."

Exercise isn't always the answer: one husband, in order to prove his great love, swam the deepest river, crossed the longest desert, and climbed the highest mountain. But his wife divorced him because he was never home.

A couple noticed that they weren't feeling as perky as they should so they decided to consult a doctor. The doctor examined them and, finding nothing organically wrong, advised them to get more exercise. So the husband went out and bought himself a set of golf clubs, and a lawn mower for his wife.

Ex-President Ford made America sports-conscious. A lot of us were unemployed—but at least we knew how to ski. . . I went to a ski resort that had three slopes: beginners, intermediates, and call-an-ambulance . . . Good skiers are made out of one mold—plaster of Paris.

The Russians are becoming great track stars—the starters are using real bullets in the starting guns . . . A lot of our politicians who are running for office—should be running for the border.

Girls who are good sports—go out more than anybody.

Sports

Sports figures are now in big business. When Reggie Jackson was caught with his pants down and put in the centerfold of the *New York Post*, he was immediately offered a multi-million-dollar deal by two magazines for *their* centerfold— *Field and Stream* and *Popular Mechanics*. He sure must have some pretty good athletic equipment.

This high-priced pitcher had one of those bad days. He made three errors and struck out four times in a row. Then he went down to the dressing room and cut himself doing the TV razor commercial—and it was an electric razor . . . The female reporter told the ball player, "Don't mind me—it's okay for you to get undressed." He said, "You first."

In the old days, an athlete was paid off with medals and silver cups. My uncle has a medal for swimming, a silver cup for golfing, and a solid gold watch for high jumping and he's not even an athlete—He owns a hock shop.

One of the great money-makers of all time in sports has got to be Muhammad Ali. The ex-champ went to a psychiatrist the other day and cried, "You've got to help me, doc. I'm developing a terrible inferiority complex. I'm beginning to think that there are other sports figures as great as I am." The doc said, "You don't have to brag about how great you are anymore—you've got it made." Ali said, "Don't misunderstand, doc, I'm just as great as I ever was. It's just that I'm more humble about it now."

Skiing is now real big business. The Attorney General's office was after one guy as a monopoly. He was operating six ski lodges and three hospitals . . . The clerk at the ski lodge said to the guest who was registering: "Just your name, address, and Blue Cross number."

My neighbor's mother was bragging that her son was in the sports repair business—fixes horse races, football games, etc.

Don't sell today's ball players short. They may be rich, but they definitely know it. This star pitcher strutted out on the mound for his first big game after signing that fabulous contract. He let fly the first pitch and the batter knocked it out of the park. He glared: "You lucky bum—you loused up my no-hitter."

There's so much football and basketball on TV now, they're thinking of passing a law: any man who watches three consecutive games can be declared legally dead by his wife. By the way, did you hear about the football player who got married? Getting into bed on the first night of his honeymoon, he slipped and hurt his back—so he sent in a substitute.

My poor neighbor thinks of nothing but sex. His idea of winter sports is making love to an Eskimo.

I'm a wrestling fan, although I realize that the only wrestling matches that aren't fixed are those in back of a car. One wrestler I knew couldn't understand why he lost the bout—he won the rehearsal.

The Post lifted the lid on the biggest scandal in horse racing history with some of the nation's leading jockeys facing indictment for fixing races . . . "They tell me playing the horses is a pretty dirty game," Sid Stone says, "but it sure cleaned me!" . . . The famous comedy pitchman tells me,

"You never realize that a dog is a man's best friend until you start betting on horses."

I asked Sid who taught him to handi up. He said, "Eddie Arcaro, Willie Shoemaker, and Raquel Welch." I said, "What could you learn from Raquel Welch?" He said, "More than I learned from Eddie Arcaro and Willie Shoemaker."

"I went to Aqueduct, that's the outdoor insane asylum," Sid told me. "I just can't stay away. You see, my hobby is horses—and that's the way they've been running, like hobby horses" . . . "A little old lady got in front of me on the fifty-dollar line and asks me where the two-dollar line is. I said, 'How do I know where the two-dollar line is?' She said, 'You keep betting those fifties and you'll soon find out where the two-dollar line is.'"

"My wife is the happiest woman now that the *Post* exposed the crooked things going on at the race tracks," Sid told me. "She is always peeved at me about my gambling. She says I got the horse habit so bad I don't even remember our wedding anniversary. I said 'Yes I do—it's two weeks before the Kentucky Derby . . .'" I saw Sid the other day looking like he lost his best pal. "Why so sad?" He said, "I had a hundred dollars stashed away to bet on the ponies—but my wife found it and blew it all on the rent and groceries."

The one day I went to the race track I met with an accident I got there safely . . . For three nights straight I dreamed about salami, bologna, and liverwurst. By pure coincidence in one race three horses by the names of Salami, Bologna and Liverwurst were running. How could I miss such a hunch? Naturally I bet on all three to win—a long shot by the name of Cold Cuts won.

Winning a lot of money at the race track is possible, even probable, but only if you're a fast horse . . . "I'm going to the race track today," my neighbor told me. "I hope to break even—I really need the money . . ." He told his wife, "One day I lose, one day I win." She said, "Why don't you play every other day?"

143

No horse can go as fast as the money you bet on him . . . My neighbor finally figured out a way to beat the first four races—he doesn't show up until the fifth.

My friend was driving to Aqueduct in a hurry when a cop stopped him and barked, "Where do you think you're going?" He said, "I'm sick!" The cop looked into the car and noticed the racing forms. "So you're sick, eh? It looks like you're going to the race track." He answered, "Oy! Is that a sickness."

The baseball season is here and with it the multimillion-dollar contracts for ball players. Would you believe Pete Rose is so rich he has an unlisted zip code? Some of the ball players now have unlisted wives. Reggie Jackson is having the dugout redone by Christian Dior.

Reggie took a girl on a picnic in his Rolls-Royce—even the paper plates were sterling silver. Would you believe he is so rich now he is sending care packages to Phil Rizzuto and Joe DiMaggio. Reggie now has four Rolls-Royces—one for each direction. As Reggie says: "I've been rich and I've been poor—believe me, rich is better . . ."

Reggie Jackson was told that he was asking a little too much money. "The President of the United States doesn't make as much money as you do." Reggie explained, "Jimmy Carter didn't have as good a season as I did."

Baseball is still the national pastime—now all we have to do is convince Lee Marvin. It was Yogi Berra, the unconscious wit of baseball, who said, "I think Little League baseball is good—it keeps the kids out of the house . . ." Yogi never knew the meaning of the word defeat—besides thousands of other words he didn't know the meaning of. Once he was trying to console his teammates: "We could still win the pennant, all we have to do is win ten out of our last 5 remaining games."

The baseball manager approached his catcher in the locker room. "Remember all those batting tips, catching tips, and base-running hints I gave you?" he asked. The ball player said, "I sure do, skipper." The manager said, "Well forget them. We just traded you."

There is only one trouble with baseball: the guy who can pitch, bat, field, and run bases better than anybody on the team—is usually sitting in the bleachers.

Football has now become the national pastime. Now go explain that to Zsa Zsa Gabor and Liz Taylor Hilton Wilding Todd Fisher Burton Burton Warner.

Football brings out the worst in women. This lady approached the perfume counter and asked the clerk: "What do you have that will compete with four hours of football on TV?"

One wife I know was so self-conscious she wouldn't go to a football game. When the players went into a huddle she thought they were talking about her.

Two football nuts were discussing the game. "My wife put her foot down last night—she said she will leave me if I don't give up following football." His pal said, "I'm so sorry." He said, "Me, too—I'm going to miss her."

I haven't played since I was injured in that college football game—I fell off the bench. But I still remember my college coach who screamed at our team after we lost the last game of the season: "For a bunch of college boys you all played like amateurs."

They say women will be playing professional football by 1981, but I don't believe it. I mean, can you picture 11 women agreeing to appear in public together—each of them wearing the same outfit?

My neighbor's wife told him if he watches as much football as he did last year, she's going to take up a new hobby— divorce.

The wife was standing on a ladder painting the ceiling. She called to her husband who was watching a football game: "If I fall off, darling," she asked, "will you call an ambulance at halftime?"

Howard Cosell told me, "It took me 20 years to realize that I know nothing about football." I said, "Then why don't you give up commentating?" He said, "I can't. It's too late—I've become an authority on the game."

The shivering wife was sitting in the stands with the screaming football maniacs all around her: "Tell me again how much fun we're having," she said to her husband, "I keep forgetting."

You know you've been watching too much football when you get into bed at night, curl up next to your wife and say, "How about it, Howard?" Football has affected our entire life style. My nephew won't even go to bed at night unless we give him a two-minute warning.

You know, sports reporters are really dumb! I mean, female reporters have won the right to go into the players' locker room, right? But not ONE male reporter has ever TRIED to go into the cheerleaders' dressing room!

Everything in football has become so specialized. Now, when Notre Dame travels they take two priests with them—the defensive chaplain and the offensive chaplain.

The Football Association is introducing a new kind of test for potential players. They take them down to Macy's during the January sales and if they can fight their way through to the ladies' spring dresses counter, they're in.

One thing about Joe Namath: he always gave a 100% performance every time he went out—and sometimes he even did that while playing football.

In the middle of the annual inundation of TV football, the man of the house failed to hear the alarm clock on Monday

146

morning, so his wife went in to wake him. "Wake up, dear, it's twenty to seven." "Whose favor?" was the sleepy reply.

Pro football is getting rougher and rougher. In fact, I understand one player has petitioned the N.F.L. to allow linebackers to take hostages . . . There is only one thing more brutal than a pro football game—and that's the price of the tickets.

The sports editor was interviewing the football coach: "What's your lineup for next season?" The coach said, "Well, as it looks now it's Johnson, Adams, and Leonard who will do the razor blade commercials, it's Hennessy, Schwartz, and Brown for the deodorants, Healy and Cross will appear for shaving cream, and Davis is slated for breakfast cereals."

The referee penalized Indian U. five yards. The incensed coach ran out on the field to protest, but it didn't help. As the referee walked the ball back five yards, the coach fumed, "You stink!" The referee paced off an additional 15 yards, looked back at the coach and said, "Okay—how do I smell from here?"

A CBS-TV crew was making a documentary of sports in a prison when the cameraman noticed that each football team had 13 men on the field. "You've got 13 men on each side," he pointed out. "You're only supposed to have 11." "That's why we're here," explained one of the convicts, "we cheat!"

It's the golf season so I thought I'd give you some advice: If you break 100, watch your golf. If you break 80—watch your business . . . I found something that can take five points off your game—it's called an eraser . . . The only time a golfer tells the truth is when he calls another golfer a liar.

Gold is a lot like taxes—you drive hard to get to the green and then wind up in a hole . . . Reading a golf manual is like reading a sex manual: It sounds great on paper, but when it comes time to making all the right moves, it's awfully hard to maintain your concentration.

Bob Hope told me: "The only trouble in playing golf with the President is the Secret Service. When you hit a ball, the trees run along with you."

When you're playing golf nothing counts like your opponent . . . "It's not that I cheat," the golfer explained, "but the lower my scores are, the better I feel—and I'm playing for my health, you know." As Hope explains: "There are three ways to improve your golf game. Take lessons, practice constantly—or start cheating."

One golfer got so disgusted with the way he was playing that he hurled his putter into the trees, then took each and every one of his clubs and smashed them into bits. He stomped into his clubhouse, took a razor blade from his locker and cut his wrists. A friend walked over and asked, "How about a game tomorrow?" The man quickly held his wrists together trying to stop the bleeding and said, "Sure, what time?"

Two alleged golfers were bragging. "Several times I almost made a hole in one," one said. "The last time I was close—I only missed it by four . . ." The other said, "I'd move heaven and earth to break 100." His friend answered, "You better concentrate on heaven—you've moved enough earth already."

It's the time of the year when the Medicare set pack up all their cares and woes, Serutan, liniment, and their golf clubs and head for Florida to visit their golf clubs, where the age of the average member is deceased . . . As George Burns puts it: "Chasing golf balls means you're too old to chase anything else . . ." Bob Hope says, "Give me my golf clubs, the fresh air, and a beautiful girl caddy—and you can keep the golf clubs and the fresh air."

The trouble with most beginners is that they stand too close to the ball—after they hit it . . .The caddy laughed at the golfer's vain attempt to contact the ball. "If you laugh at me again," the man shouted, "I'll hit you over the head with this club." The caddy admitted, "Maybe you could at that—it *is* a little larger than the ball."

A new golfer was playing a short hole. With a full swing, he gave the ball a mighty wallop. The ball hit a tree, bounced off and hit another tree, then ricocheted onto a rock and finally landed on the green, about three inches from the hole. He looked at it in disgust and said, "If I had only hit just a little harder."

I regard golf as an expensive way of playing marbles . . . Golf was once a rich man's sport, but it now has millions of poor players . . . As soon as a businessman takes up golf, he becomes an executive . . .

You meet some strange people when you play golf. I was getting ready to start out with a threesome the other day when a fellow came up with a putter over his shoulder and said, "Would you like to make it a foursome?" We said, "Sure." And then he said, "I don't have any balls." So we gave him a ball, and right away he drove it into a lake hazard. So we gave him three more balls, which he drove into the lake. Finally, when he asked for another ball, I said, "Hey, mister, these balls cost a buck and a half apiece." And he said, "Well, if you can't afford to play golf, don't play it."

Bob Hope calls Jackie Gleason the miracle golfer: "When he puts the ball where he can hit it—he can't see it. And when he puts the ball where he can see it—he can't hit it!" . . . Bob asked his priest, "Will I sin if I play golf on the Sabbath?" The father answered, "The way you play—it's a sin to play any day."

After playing his worst game, the unhappy golfer asked his partner what he thought he should give his caddy. The other golfer shrugged. "Have you ever thought of giving him your clubs?"

A fair golfer is one who putts after 18 holes or 90 strokes—whichever comes first. I'm thinking of giving up golf—I can't break 90 even when I cheat.

I'm not exactly a great golfer. I have no particular handicap—I'm all handicap. I called up a friend and asked him to play. He said: "Sorry—we already have a threesome."

This was really a golf nut. He was just about to tee off on the first hole when a beautiful girl came running up to him in a gorgeous bridal outfit. The golfer waved her away and said: "Sylvia—I told you—only if it rains."

Two golfanatics were talking at the clubhouse and one said: "Did you hear about Frank killing his wife?" And the other asks, "In how many strokes?"

By the time a man can afford to lose a ball—he can't hit that far.

Sammy Davis was asked about his handicap when he played golf with Bob Hope. He said: "I'm black, I'm Jewish, and I have one eye—any other questions?"

Sign at the Glasgow National Golf Club: "Do not pick up lost balls until they have stopped rolling."

Golf has made more liars out of the American people than the income tax.

"Let me say this about your game, mister," the caddy said. "I wouldn't say you were the worst golfer I have ever seen on this course—but I've seen places today that I have never seen before."

Many a man whose doctor advised him to play golf has an instructor who advises him to quit.

The Social Scene: Cocktail Parties & Drinking, Suburbia, Apartment Life, and Fashion

If you want to know who's doing what and to whom and with what, go to a cocktail party. If they don't know, they'll start a whole new plot for you . . . Most people go to cocktail parties to gossip and drink—it's the gossip that drives them to drink.

If they don't start the gossip—they will sure keep it from dying down . . . The way some people keep a secret is by refusing to say who it was that told it to them.

The catty one was murdering the lady standing at the bar in the country club. "You must know her very well," one listener noted. "Well, I don't know her to speak to," she said, "only to talk about."

My neighbor's wife never repeats gossip—she starts it . . . She'll never tell a lie—if the truth will cause more damage . . . She's the kind who likes to listen to both sides of an argument—but only if it's on a party line . . . She was driving home from the party with her husband when she said to him, "Well, you certainly did make a fool of yourself tonight. I just hope nobody realized you were sober."

I'll take a compliment from anybody. This lady at one cocktail party told me that drinking made me good-looking. I told her I wasn't drinking—she said *she* was.

153

There's a difference between a drunk and an alcoholic. The drunk doesn't have to go to meetings—he goes to cocktail parties . . . So remember, when a man drinks too much at a cocktail party, he becomes tight. When a woman does—she becomes loose.

Show me a man at a cocktail party who can eat, drink, and be merry—and I'll show you a fat, grinning drunk.

The great social phenomenon of the age is the cocktail party. When I was a kid, the cocktail party was the corner candy store or the fire escape and the gossip was called B.S. . . . At today's cocktail party, next to the ice cubes, the most important commodity is still B.S. . . . The idea at these things is: Don't talk about yourself—it will be done when you leave.

People at cocktail parties don't always believe everything they hear, but often repeat it just to be on the safe side . . . Some people believe anything you tell them if you whisper it . . . This shark was so tired, she could hardly keep her mouth open: "There's no use you should keep asking me for details," she told her listeners, "in fact, I've already told you more than I heard myself."

"My dears," gushed the hostess, "my resolution this year is never to repeat gossip—so for heaven's sake listen carefully the first time . . ." "Mildred got mixed up with you-know-who and they went to what's-his-name's house to get you-know-what and she and what-do-you-call-him got caught with the what-do-you-call-it and you should see what happened to you-know-who on account of you-know-why—I told you the story before?" She said, "Yeah, but this is the first time I heard all the details."

The things you overhear at cocktail parties: Alan King: "A suburbanite believes in these inalienable rights—life, liberty, and the pursuit of his neighbor's wife" . . . Marcello Mastroianni: "Once they call you a Latin lover, you're in real trouble—women expect an Oscar performance every time you just nibble them on the neck."

154

Two women, former neighbors, met over the buffet after a separation of several years. "Really," purred one, "I would hardly have known you; you look so much older." The other meowed, "I wouldn't have recognized you either, except for your hat and dress."

Two committee ladies were inhaling the hors d'oeuvres: "I gained so much weight," sighed one, "I could kill myself." The other suggested, "Why don't you take arsenic?" The first said, "Too many calories."

Society is full of unemployed titles who have nothing but snob appeal . . . A snob is a person who only wants to know people who don't want to know him . . . This Duke something-or-other is such a royal pain, the other day he asked the liquor store to recommend the proper wine to go with a TV dinner.

It takes all kinds of people to make a world and the snob is glad she's not one of them . . . A society put-on is one whose grandfather made money and who therefore refuses to associate with persons who have made it themselves . . . Did you ever notice that in society, nobody arrives until everybody else has?

Two older society gals, poor but snobbish, were talking about a matrimonial prospect: "He's got plenty of money," one said, "but isn't he too old to be termed eligible?" The other said, "Dahling, he's too eligible to be termed old."

Two society ladies were talking at tea. One is so classy she has monogrammed garbage. "Breeding is everything, is it not?" one growled. The other said, "No—but it's lots of fun."

He's such a snob—he won't get a suntan because he says it would clash with his blue blood.

I made the mistake of asking my librarian to help trace my roots—She discovered that one of my ancestors had an overdue book, and I had to pay the fine.

They are quite a society couple. They live in a restricted area—nobody in their neighborhood has a home they can afford. She finally asked for a divorce because of her husband's bad table manners. "He always holds his little pinky out when he holds a cup of tea." The judge said, "Lady, in society it's proper to hold out your little pinky when you're drinking tea." She said, "With the tea bag hanging from it?"

Twice a year Dean Martin goes to the Red Cross and donates a fifth of blood . . . The doctor told him if he didn't stop drinking, he'd lose his hearing. Dean said, "I told him the stuff I've been drinking is a lot better than the stuff I've been hearing."

This poor soul ordered a martini, "extra rare." The bartender corrected, "You mean extra dry." He said, "No, extra rare— I'm having it for my dinner."

Jackie Gleason asked the bartender for a martini, "consisting of six parts gin and one part vermouth." The bartender asked, "would you like a slice of lemon peel twisted in it?" Gleason snarled, "If I want a lemonade, I'll ask for it."

Two men planned to go hunting. "I'll bring the hunting paraphernalia," said one, "and you bring the provisions." The provisions man arrived with one loaf of bread and four bottles of whiskey. "Fine thing," snapped the other. "I leave it to you and what happens? You bring a loaf of bread and four bottles of whiskey. Now what are we going to do with all that bread?"

The Chinese can't understand our drinking habits at all. One Chinese visitor told me, "Funny people, you Americans. You put gin in your drink to warm you up, then ice to keep you cool, you say, 'here's to you'—and then you drink it yourself."

Red Skelton says: "A beer is about all I can drink or I get asthma and people think I'm passionate." Red says, "We don't have water enough for beer in California. The alfalfa's so short, we have to lather it to cut it. We go to a lake and drink the water bed."

Teetotalers tell you that whiskey has killed more people than bullets. Dean said, "That's true—but I'd rather be full of whiskey than full of bullets."

I won't say Dean Martin has a drinking problem, but his major concern in life is what wine goes with whiskey.

I knew he was loaded when he got into the elevator and told the operator to take him to the airport—in a hurry.

This drunk staggered up to the hotel clerk and demanded another room. The clerk said, "But sir, you have the best room in the place." The man said stubbornly, "I want another room and I want it quick." So the clerk said to the bellboy, "Get this gentleman out of 505 and put him in 508." The drunk started to walk away and the clerk said, "Would you mind telling me why you don't like 505?" And the drunk said, "Well, for one thing, it's on fire."

George Jean Nathan said, "I drink to make other people interesting." Dean Martin says, "There's only one thing worse than a drinking man—and that's a man who doesn't drink."

My neighbor says his drinking habits don't agree with his love life. His girl says she won't marry him when he's drunk and he won't marry her when he's sober.

The two drunks were fishing on a dock when an alligator nipped one of them on the foot. So the guy screams, "An alligator just bit off one of my toes!" and his friend says, "Which one?" And the guy says, "How do I know—all alligators look alike to me."

Phil Harris says, "Actually, it only takes one drink to get me loaded—I can't recall if it's the 12th or the 13th!"

There are two kinds of people at cocktail parties: Those who want to leave early and those who don't—the trouble is they are usually married to each other.

Hear no evil, see no evil, speak no evil—and you'll never be a success at a cocktail party . . . The only redeeming feature of a gossip is that she always talks about somebody more interesting than herself.

Two women at a party noticed a familiar face at the other end of the room: "Do you see who I see? It's Helen. Tell me, do you believe that terrible story about her?" The other said, "Yes—what is it?"

I met a friend I haven't seen for a long time at one party. Of course I wanted to know how he was feeling. "Terrible," he explained, "I have hardening of the arteries, high blood pressure, dizziness, arthritis, bronchitis . . ." I told him how sorry I was to hear about all his miseries. "What have you been doing?" I asked. "Same thing I've been doing for years," he said, "Still selling health foods."

Remember, when you are telling your troubles to people, half of them aren't interested and the other half are glad to see you're finally getting what's coming to you.

Bernard Meltzer cornered me at a literary tea and lectured: "Remember, when trouble starts, take it like a man—blame it on your wife."

I have one big problem with New Year's Eve: I misplace things—like New Year's Day. I'm not going out on New Year's Eve this year. Why should I spend all that money on some thing I won't even remember?

I won't say that my neighbor throws wild parties, but no one is admitted without signing the register—with your name, address, and next of kin.

My neighbor really goes wild on New Year's Eve. I'll never forget last year. He went tearing around town, honking his horn, weaving in and out of traffic, running red lights—thank goodness he wasn't in his car at the time.

I never drink on New Year's Eve. That's amateur night—like the cop who asked the drunk where he thought he was going. "I'm coming home from a Noo Yearsh Eve party," he stammered. "Are you kidding?" the cop growled. "New Year's was three weeks ago." The drunk answered, "I know, that'sh why I figured I better be getting home."

New Year's Eve the drunk staggered out of the bar and fumbled for his keys in front of his car. The cop said, "You're not going to drive in that condition, are you?" "You're damn right I am—I'm too drunk to walk."

They promised to meet in the same bar on New Year's Eve ten years later. So, ten years to the hour one of them walked in and sure enough there was his pal on a stool. "I never thought," he said, "that day when we left this bar I'd really see you here today." "Who left?" hiccuped his pal.

"Love thy neighbor," is the anthem of the suburbs. One guy on Long Island suspected his wife and sent a letter to his good-looking neighbor: "I shall expect you to appear at my office this afternoon to explain why you have been carrying on with my wife." He received a prompt reply: "Your circular letter received and comments duly noted. Thanks for the invitation—I shall be glad to attend the caucus."

My neighbor confided to me: "I told my wife the truth. I told her I was seeing a psychiatrist—and she told me the truth: She's seeing a psychiatrist, two plumbers, and a bartender."

"I wonder if you can locate my husband for me," a lady just arrived in heaven asked wistfully of Saint Peter. "What's his name?" said Saint Peter. "Bill Smith," said the lady. "My goodness, madam," Saint Peter declared patiently. "We have about four million Bill Smiths up here. Can't you think of some distinguishing characteristic?" "Well," mused the lady, "I do remember that just before he died, my Bill told me that if I ever was unfaithful to him, he'd turn in his grave." "That

159

makes it simple," laughed Saint Peter. "Boy, go out and page Whirling Willie."

Horowitz bragged about his wife's beauty and charm. "You mean," a friend said, "that you don't know your wife has four lovers?" He said, "Well, I'd rather have 20 percent in a good deal than 100 percent in a lousy one."

Irving received a call from Sam: "I have two passes to the hockey game—I'll take you . . ." Irving said, "I can't—Stravinsky is playing tonight." Sam called the next night with passes for a basketball game. Irving said, "Can't make it—Stravinsky is playing tonight." Sam said, "Wait a minute—what does this guy Stravinsky play?" Irving said, "Who knows? I never even met him. I don't know what he plays, but when Stravinsky is playing—I'm playing with his wife."

Sylvia and Myrtle, two pretty young housewives, were talking over lunch: "I'm ashamed to admit it," said one, "but I caught my husband making love." The other said, "Why let that bother you? I got mine the same way."

"Now as I understand it," the attorney began sympathetically, "every night when you returned home from work, instead of finding your wife alone and waiting for you, you found a different man hiding in the closet . . ." "Yes, that's right" . . . "And this of course, caused you untold anguish and unhappiness . . ." "Why sure! I never had any room to hang up my clothes."

An American city is a place where by the time you're finished paying for your home in the suburbs—the suburbs have moved twenty miles farther out.

Suburbia—where the houses are farther apart—and the payments are closer together . . .

One real estate broker called the actor with the perfect home in the suburbs. A short drive to Broadway, a great place to entertain, no worry about civilians pestering you: "But there is some good news and some bad news." The actor asked,

"What's the good news?" The broker said, "Well, we can get that beautiful mansion you're so crazy about for only $210,000." The actor was ecstatic. "Wonderful—now what's the bad news?" "They want $2,000 down."

There are two kinds of suburbanites: those who talk about how rich they're gonna be—and those who talk about how rich they used to be.

There's a new perfume that's big in suburbia that smells like chlorine—for people who want you to think they have a swimming pool.

I'm strictly a city lover, but you have to admire the American spirit. Where else but in America can somebody borrow the $10,000 down payment from a relative, get a $60,000 first mortgage, a $30,000 second mortgage—and be called a home-owner . . . America is the only country where you can have two cars, a house, a boat, and a camper, without owning any of them . . .

A family I know lived happily in a little apartment in New York, but decided to move to a big house in the country. Last week I saw the 12-year-old son and asked, "How do you like your new house?" He said, "Oh, we love it. I have my own room, my sisters have their own rooms, but poor mom—she's still in with dad."

Having a home in the suburbs is a problem of location: It's usually on the outskirts of your income . . . My neighbor wanted to try the suburbs. He says, "We were offered a house in our price range—but it was in Cambodia." He explained later: "A suburbanite husband is just a gardener with sex privileges."

One couple furnished a 12-room house with premiums redeemed for soap coupons. They showed me around, proudly telling me how many coupons each table, chair, bed, and carpet cost. At the end of the tour I said, "But you've only shown me five rooms—what about the other seven?" He said, "Oh those? That's where we keep the soap."

161

Don't laugh at people who live in the suburbs: You may get a raise some day and live there yourself . . . If you want to write something that will live forever—sign a mortgage.

One suburbanite told me: "I just paid the insurance on my home and it's pretty silly—I had to sell the house to do it."

There's the sad tale about the two-story house—the real estate man sold him one story before he built it and another one afterward . . . The agent squelched one newly married couple: "The only house available in your price range is now occupied by a party of robins."

The new homes in the country advertise: "Everything is built in"—except the price. That's jacked up . . . This one architect was having a tough time with a prospective home-builder: "Can't you give me *some* idea of the type of house you want to build?" The man said, "Well, all I know is that it must go with an antique doorknob my wife bought."

A good friend of mine lived in a very fashionable part of Long Island, but he wanted a change. So he called a real estate agent and told him to put his home up for sale. The next Saturday he read the "For sale" ad in the *New York Post* and called the agent immediately: "I'm not going to sell my house—your ad convinced me it's just the kind of house I want."

It's almost impossible to get a hotel room or an apartment in New York. They call them high-rise apartments because the rents are sky-high . . . They are putting up all those new apartment houses now with every modern convenience—except low rent.

And they are so particular when you want an apartment . . . The apartment house manager looked at the prospective tenant suspiciously. "I must remind you that we do not rent to children, we do not tolerate cats, dogs, and parrots. No piano playing and no TV after 10 P.M. Is that clear?" "Yes," said the tenant, "but I have a confession. I eat celery from time to time."

I lived in one of those apartment houses that doesn't allow children and they are very strict about it. One of the tenants is now in her fifteenth month.

Modern apartments are built on the principle that half as much room should cost twice as much money . . . Ken Friedman told me, "I have a three-room apartment. That's a living room, bedroom, and a mailbox. I spend most of my time in the mailbox—because that's the room with the window." Ken says: "My apartment is so small the refrigerator opens in."

Landlords now have the upper hand. The best way to get your landlord to paint your apartment is to move out. Henny Youngman says, "My apartment has so many windows that I now get cross-pollution . . ." Soupy Sales called his landlord and told him his apartment had terrible acoustics. The landlord insisted, "We caught them all long before you moved in."

I read an article in some science magazine that by 1983 they will be able to heat an entire apartment house with only one lump of coal. Are they kidding? I got a landlord who is trying to do it now.

Many of today's apartments have what are called "living rooms." In the old days they were walk-in closets. The ideal apartment is large enough to keep your wife from going home to mother—and small enough to keep her mother from coming to you.

A woman used to go to a doctor to see if she could have children—now she goes to her landlord.

The man asked the superintendent of the building: "Do you have suitable accommodations where I can put up with my wife?"

The two housewives from the same floor in the apartment house were having a feud. Sara claims Myrtle never returned the soup pot she lent her. Myrtle's reply was a gem of logic:

"In the first place I never took a pot from you. In the second place it was an old pot. And in the third place, I gave it back to you in better condition than when I took it from you!"

The woman was telling her neighbor in the tenement house that she was moving: "We're going to be living in a better neighborhood soon." Her neighbor volunteered, "So are we." She asked, "You mean you are moving too?" The neighbor said, "No—we're staying here."

My neighbor told me, "My landlord has promised he won't convert the place into a condominium. He's just making me buy my bathroom . . ." My neighbor says he told the landlord the apartment had roaches—"So he raised my rent another $20 a month for keeping pets!"

And every twenty minutes they change the rents. New York is the only place you can go broke sleeping. . . . At these rents, nobody wants to go out—they stay in their rooms and watch them . . .

Lee Tully told me they raised the rent in his apartment. He asked the landlord the reason. He said, "We put music in the elevators." Lee said, "I live on the second floor—how long can I dance?"

My uncle Morris says he never had luck with any apartment in New York City: "I remember my first apartment—I just got married and I carried my wife over the threshold. She saw the apartment and said, 'Don't put me down.'"

Hotels in this town are going up as fast as the rates . . . Now all we need are people who can afford them . . . The *New Helmsley Palace* is so high class, that even Mr. Helmsley has to use the service entrance . . . You sit at the bar and you order a highball—they bring it to you in prescription glasses . . . Even the single rooms have gold tubs—one Texan took a bath and left a 14-karat ring . . . That Helmsley is so rich he has Swiss money in American banks.

The Grand Hyatt is a really big hotel. How big is it? Well, calling room service is long distance . . . Before the Trump organization took it over, it used to be the Commodore. And talking about room service—it was so slow, when I ordered breakfast, I had to leave a forwarding address . . .

The new *Harley Hotel* is near the U.N. and grabs the international set . . . In that lobby, English is a second language . . . There are so many foreigners in the hotel, you aren't allowed to drink the water . . .

The new *Milford Plaza* attracts the traveling salesman, and, naturally, my traveling salesman-type jokes: Since the hotel is on 8th Avenue, the new arrival was out on the street shopping the market, looking for a particular piece of merchandise, preferably marked down. So, he approached one little beauty on the corner and asked, "Do you speak English?" She said, "A leetle beet." He asked, "A little bit, eh? How much?" She said, "Twenty-five dollar."

There's one hotel in town that's strictly for cheaters. In fact, when a couple registers, they sign in as Mr. and Mrs. To-Whom-It-May-Concern . . . One guy followed his wife there and he broke into the room and found her making love to his best friend. "You'll pay for this," he shouted. The friend said calmly, "Are you on American Express? I never leave home without it."

The mini is coming back, but now you will have a choice of three kinds of miniskirts: mini, micro, and don't bend over . . . Those skirts keep getting higher all the time—I wonder what they'll be up to next? The skirts are getting shorter and the neckline lower—I'd like to be there when they meet.

With today's fashions, you can't tell if a girl is wearing a high miniskirt or a low lobster bib . . . To me, a miniskirt is a calculated risqué . . . It's definitely not for the woman who came into fashion too late—by twenty years and forty pounds.

Long skirts don't bother me—I have a good memory. But to tell you the truth, minis make men more polite. Did you ever see a man get on a bus *before* a girl with a mini? . . . They say long skirts pick up a lot of germs—you should see what the short skirts pick up . . . Those minis will never go out of style—they will look just as ridiculous year after year.

One thing—women will be wearing the same thing in brassieres this year . . . I can't believe the fashions. The first time I saw a woman in a split skirt, I offered her a safety pin . . . I can't believe some of those way-out fashions women wear—I feel like a peeping Tom just walking down the street.

The slit skirt creates some serious problems for drunks. Now when you stagger out of a bar, the lady leaning against the lamppost *could* be your wife . . . Actually, I find those slit skirts very pleasing—not to mention teasing.

Of course, it really doesn't do anything for most women. When my neighbor wears her slit skirt, I can peer through the slit and see her sexy varicose veins . . . She not only had a slit skirt, but a slit slip and slit pantyhose . . . My secretary gets her fashion trends a little confused—yesterday she wore a slit miniskirt.

The pretty young thing walked over to the salesman in the department store wearing earrings longer than her dress: "This dress is too long for me—do you have anything shorter?" He said, "Try the belt department."

The most attractive thing about the latest fashions for women is that it won't last . . . Fashion by any other name would be just as ridiculous . . . If women dressed to please men, they'd dress a hell of a lot faster.

"I would like a mink coat," the wife demanded. The husband tried to reason with her: "But you've only worn that one I gave you two years." She said, "You forget the eight years the mink wore it."

She was using a soft, feminine material to make a dress. "See," she said, holding the dress up to herself to show her husband. "Won't it be pretty when it's finished?" The husband exclaimed, "But you can see right through it." She said, "Not when I'm in it . . ." The designer of see-through blouses suggested this advertising jingle: "I'll be seeing you—in all the old familiar places."

My neighbor's wife always wants to buy a new outfit every time they're invited out. He thought he'd play a big joke on her once and accepted an invite to a nudist wedding. The joke was on him—she spent $1,500 on a body lift.

Have you stopped to think how styles have changed? Fifty years ago women wore bathing suits down to their ankles. Twenty-five years ago they wore them down to their knees. Ten years ago they wore them down to their hips—now they don't even wear them down to the water.

If a girl has never been married, the wedding gown should be white. If she has been married before, she wears a blue gown. If she's been married for the third time, a white dress trimmed with blue. I can just see Zsa Zsa Gabor at her next wedding—she's going to look silly coming down that aisle in a crazy quilt.

Fashion is a personal thing: Phyllis Diller is the only girl I know who wears prescription underwear . . . Sophia Loren says: "I don't like loose dresses—tents are for Boy Scouts . . ." Cindy notes: "I saw some of those new bikini fashions —why, I have earrings that cover more than that . . ."

I like to go to Paris to see the fashions—the exotic perfumes, the see-through blouses, the tight jeans—but that's enough about the boys. Now let's talk about the girl's fashions . . . Designer jeans are great—if you don't care about blood pressure below the waist.

The décolletage of some of the new fashions is going a little far, when a girl can reach into the top of her dress to put money in her stocking.

This actually happened at a military ball in Washington. One girl in a very low-cut dress said to her friend in the plunging neckline: "Don't dance with the general—his medals are cold."

You can't believe how my wife likes to shop. She's the only woman I know who has to send her credit card to the shop for repairs.

My wife buys so many gowns from Paris on our budget that her clothing allowance is listed as "Foreign Aid."

My wife will buy anything marked down. Last week she brought home an escalator.

My wife knows you can't buy happiness—so she charges it.

Mickey Freeman's wife went to the bank to cash her husband's paycheck. "It needs an endorsement," the teller explained. The wife thought for a moment, then wrote on the back of the check, "Mickey is a wonderful husband."

My neighbor brags about his wife: "She stuck with me through all the troubles I never would have gotten into—if I didn't marry her in the first place."

Girl's fashions may change—but their designs are the same.

I'm for women's rights. I think women should be equal to men—even though they lose some of their power.

Some husbands have a point. "My wife spends all day preparing for dinner," one guy told me, "not working—preparing to go out."

A woman spends the first part of life shopping for a husband—and the rest of her life shopping for everything else.

The two girls were shopping for a man on the beach. The muscleman passed by and one said, "That's my kind of man." The other said, "I don't know. I had a friend who

168

married a man who owned a two-car garage—but he just keeps a bicycle in it."

A dress shop received this note: "Dear sir: You have not yet delivered that maternity dress I ordered. Please cancel the order—my delivery was faster than yours."

A woman trying on a mink coat said to the salesgirl: "If my husband doesn't like it, will you promise to refuse to take it back?"

The State of the Nation: Oil, Business, Taxes, Inflation, and Other Matters

I bought a Rolls-Royce and paid cash—the gas I had to finance . . .

One gas station has a sign outside that says, "We collect taxes, federal, state, and local—we also sell gas as a sideline . . ." I never could figure out those gas stations. In the office the cash register is wide open, the safe is wide open—but the men's room is locked.

"Who cares about the price of gasoline?" my neighbor was crying. "At today's prices, who can afford a car?" . . . My neighbor told his wife, "I've just discovered oil on our property." She said, "Wonderful, now we can buy a new car." He said, "No, we'd better get the old one repaired—that's where the oil is coming from."

I have no sympathy for the oil industry. I mean, when was the last time you saw a poor millionaire?

One Congressman came up with a great idea: "Instead of burning precious fuel to generate electricity, why don't the electric companies burn something worthless, something they already have plenty of—money!"

At the present price of gasoline, they really shouldn't call them oil tankers—clipper ships would be more accurate . . . Inflation is getting so bad that, when one teenager drove his broken-down car into the gas station and asked for a dollar's worth of gas, the attendant sprayed a little behind his ear.

They talk about cars getting smaller. Not so. Take my gas tank; it used to hold six dollars worth—now it holds $23. . . . I got a close friend who owns a gas station. All I have to do is bring my friend a bunch of blue chips and a set of dishes and he sells me all the gas I want.

Bob Hope told me he drove into a gas station and the attendant refused to fill up his tank. He said, "What do you expect me to do for gas?" The guy said, "Try Rolaids." Bob told the gas station attendant to give him a dollar's worth of gas—so he let him sniff the pump.

I'm not saying the prices being charged for gasoline are criminal, but the other day after a service attendant filled up my tank, I saw him wipe his fingerprints off the nozzle!

Sure the oceans are becoming full of oil spills. My neighbor looks at the bright side of things: "Last year I was able to feed my family and heat my home on 200 pounds of flounder."

The oil companies are sure ripping us off. For years they gave us the tiger in the tank—but now they're just giving us a lot of bull . . . Wouldn't you know it! No sooner do I buy an economy car—they stop making economy gasoline . . . I knew I'd have to sacrifice something to pay for my new car, but I never dreamed it would be gasoline!

My old friend Vic Oliver had the greatest definition of the value of money: "If a man runs after money, he's money mad; if he keeps it, he's a capitalist; if he spends it, he's a playboy; if he doesn't get it, he's a ne'er-do-well; if he doesn't try to get it, he lacks ambition. If he gets it without working for it, he's a parasite; and if he accumulates it after a lifetime of hard work, people call him a fool who never got anything out of life."

People who lose sleep over the stock market are lucky—I lose money. The reason the stock market shuts down on the weekend: It gives the investors' hair a chance to grow out . . . A stockbroker advises what to do with money you wouldn't have if you had followed his advice . . . Now I'm in real trouble. First my laundry called and said they lost my shirt and then my broker said the same thing.

The only thing I've learned about the stock market is that you have to be patient—and the way it's been going lately, I'm going to become one . . . I'm the only guy that buys stocks under the counter. I wish they wouldn't talk about a recession—I still owe a fortune from the boom. The only thing that annoys me is that when you buy, the broker makes a profit—when you get scared and sell, the broker makes a profit. My broker has only one problem—how to look sad with a smile on his face.

I like the story of the two brokers who were having a martini and one said, "Let's talk about something else besides stocks and bonds for a change." The other said, "Fine, let's talk about women." The first said, "Good idea—common or preferred?"

Love affairs and stocks have one thing in common. They are easier to get into than out of . . . My neighbor told his wife. "Remember that stock I was going to retire on at 55? Well, my retirement age is now 350."

My family wasn't affected by the stock market crash of 1929—they went broke in 1928 . . . Someday we'll find that it hurts just as much to lose your money in the stock market under the S.E.C. as it did in the old unethical days . . . I don't know what's happening on Wall Street today, but my broker just moved his office to a crap table in Atlantic City.

Morris Lamer at Herzfeld and Stern got a call from one of his clients: "Get me 500 shares of A T & T," he pleaded, "and when I get even—sell me out . . ." I won't say I've made some bad investments lately, but yesterday I caught Mr. Whipple trying to squeeze my stock portfolio.

The man who butts his head against the stock market—soon learns why its called Wall Street . . . Wall Street is made up of three types of investors—bulls, bears, and asses . . . Personally, I own a great deal of penny stock—too bad I bought it for three dollars.

Everybody "plays" the stock market. My neighbor bought some stock for his old age, and it worked—within a month he was an old man . . . As far as I'm concerned, I'm neither a bull or a bear—I'm chicken . . . Morey Amsterdam says, "I'm out of the stock market—I'm waiting for the IRS to go public."

I don't want to say I don't trust my broker. But the other day I went to see him and he was wearing a stocking mask . . .

I know a fella made a fortune on the market: $100,000, to be exact. He slipped on a grape in a supermarket—and sued.

Will Rogers's advice is still the best: "Don't gamble. Buy some good stock. Hold it till it goes up and then sell it. If it doesn't go up—don't buy it."

I went to meet my broker for lunch, and he was sitting in the park with two brown bags on the bench. I said, "I can't believe it, two brown bags and that's lunch?" He said, "What lunch? This is my luggage."

The only difference between the current stock market and the Titanic is that the Titanic had a band.

You must look on the positive side of Wall Street. Like the sound, secure investments of today are the tax losses of tomorrow.

My stockbroker has figured out a way for me to beat the income tax—he gives me all losers.

The big thing on Wall Street today are the investment clubs. For those of you who are naive—an investment club is a way to lose your money by parliamentary procedure.

Mother decided Junior was getting pretty big and perhaps Daddy should have a heart-to-heart talk with him. The old man could run things pretty good on the stock exchange, but this was a delicate task. Finally, after four or five martinis, he took his son into the library and started, "Son, I'm going to tell you about the bulls and the bears."

I'll never understand the stock market. Some of my stocks just went from the financial page to the comics.

Our tax refunds will take a while this year—first, Congress has to find out if it's legal to give money to Americans.

My hospital has four different rates: For $300 a day, you're in a room with a water bed filled with chicken soup; for $175 a day, you're in a semiprivate room; for $90 a day, you're in a ward; and for $29.95, you're the top person in a wheelchair!

My neighbor says he never gets any breaks. He tried to file for bankruptcy, but they told him his credit wasn't good enough.

I never have luck in investments. If I bought stock in IBM, the abacus would make a comeback.

My uncle just bought a very expensive home in the suburbs. It has four bedrooms, three baths, a den—and a tiny office where the man from the finance company lives.

You've got to work faithfully in your business. If you work diligently eight hours a day and don't worry, in time you will become the boss—and work 12 hours a day and do all the worrying.

The man most likely to succeed is invariably the boss's son. This young business executive gave an interview to the *New York Post* and bragged, "Those early days were tough, but I put my shoulder to the wheel, rolled up my sleeves, gritted my teeth, and borrowed another $700,000 from my father."

My mechanic says a valve job on my car will run $395! $395? I wonder who's doing the operation—Dr. Christian Barnaard?

It was Sam Goldwyn who first said it: "I don't want any yes-men around me. I want everyone to tell me the truth—even if it costs them their jobs!"

The New York Stock Exchange is the largest dance hall in the world. Where else can you see over a thousand people on one floor, all doing *the hustle*!

I just received some shocking news. My former stockbroker is in jail. He's doing 11-3/4 to 19-1/8 for stock fraud.

Aften ten years in the business, my stockbroker has learned to do one thing well—apologize.

There is a teenage investment group—they trust no stock over thirty.

You have to give most American families a lot of credit—they can't get along without it. Credit cards have become a way of life. It's getting to a point where the only people who carry cash these days are counterfeiters and toll collectors . . .

Education is a wonderful thing—if you couldn't sign your name, you'd have to pay cash . . . I'm so used to using credit cards that when I bought something for cash the other day, I signed all the dollar bills . . . It's credit everywhere. My neighbor got held up, and the thief asked for his credit cards. What got my neighbor mad was when the crook dragged him over to a pay phone, took a dime from him and called to see if his credit was good.

My neighbor told me, "My wife spends so much money it's driving me crazy." I asked, "Why don't you talk to her about it?" He said, "To tell the truth, it's easier to talk to the creditors . . ." Most department stores are willing to give a woman credit for what her husband earns . . . He figured out a way to cut down his wife's expenses—he hid all her credit cards.

Sal Richards says: "When I got married, my wife figured the only way we could survive was to apply for credit cards. The first card she got was the Express Card. Express is the right name—it takes you directly from your house to the poorhouse . . . Then she got the Everything Card. And that's exactly what she did—went out and bought everything . . . We couldn't pay any of these things, so we started writing checks. We had so many checks returned that our bank bounced. I think we were the only people in our neighborhood with a live-in sheriff."

My uncle had barely paid off his mortgage on the house when he mortgaged it again to buy a car, and not too long after that he borrowed money to build a garage. His banker hesitated and said, "If I do make this new loan, how will you buy gas for the car?" My uncle said, "It seems to me that a fellow who owns a big house, a car, and a garage should be able to get credit for gas."

These days if somebody pays you in cash you get suspicious. You think maybe his credit is no good . . . Credit cards are what people use when they discover that money can't buy everything . . . Credit cards have made buying easier but paying harder . . . Using a credit card is a convenient way to spend money you wish you had.

A little old lady walked into the credit department of American Express and demanded, "I don't care to bandy words with underlings about my overdrawn account—take me to your computer."

The only things you can't buy nowadays with a credit card is money.

I wish people wouldn't tell me that I look just the way I did 30 years ago—so does the dollar.

There is plenty of money around these days. The trouble is—everyone owes it to someone else. I know a guy whose credit rating is so bad—they won't even accept his money.

Running into debt isn't so bad—it's running into creditors that hurts. "If you didn't intend to pay your bill," the tailor said angrily, "why the hell did you haggle over the price so much?" He said, "I didn't want you to lose so much."

Did you ever stop to think that the income tax is just the government's method of spring cleaning.

It is well known that George Washington never told a lie. Of course, he lived in the days before the I.R.S. audit.

There's only one thing to be said about the wages of sin. It's about the only wage the government doesn't tax.

I just found out what happens to little boys who tell lies—they grow up to be tax accountants.

Work may not be as hard as it used to be, but it certainly is a lot more taxing. We've never had it so good—or taken away from us so fast.

In filling out your income tax returns—let an accountant (instead of your conscience) be your guide.

An accountant is a man hired to explain that you didn't make the money you did.

Motto in filling out your income tax: "It is better to give then to receive—and safer, too." I know a man who wrote a letter to the Internal Revenue Service: "I haven't been able to sleep since I cheated on last year's income tax. Enclosed please find one thousand dollars. If I find I still can't sleep—I'll send you the rest of the money."

They're pretty clever those I.R.S. guys. First they put a big tax on liquor. Then they raise all other taxes—to drive people to drink.

We may not admire everything about the government—but we do have to hand it to the Internal Revenue Service. Like the man who explained to his accountant: "I'm sure I could live within my income—if Uncle Sam could live without it."

If you don't think there are two sides to every story—just listen to the guy discuss his finances with friends and then with the tax collector.

You think you have problems? We have a plumber who no longer makes house calls.

My electric bill is so huge I had to get a second mortgage on my fuse box.

If at first you don't succeed—work it off as a tax deduction: "You just can't come in here like this and ask for a raise," the boss said to his newest employee. "You mut work yourself up." The employee replied, "But I did—Look, I'm trembling all over."

Now I know why I could never keep up with the Joneses— they were just indicted for income tax evasion.

The I.R.S. claims their forms are so simple any three-year-old could fill them out. That would be great if three-year-olds had any income to file a return for.

I had an accountant one year who saved me $4,000. He did a tremendous amount of business. He did so well he had to relocate. Now he's in Brazil.

One lady called the I.R.S. and asked if birth control pills were deductible. "Only if they don't work," she was told.

If you want to see a surprised face—go to the I.R.S. and demand an audit.

The average man pays a luxury tax on his billfold, an income tax on the stuff he puts into it—and a sales tax whenever he takes anything out.

A man owes it to himself to become a success. Once he's successful—he owes it to the income tax collector.

Anybody who thinks the best things in life are free—just hasn't been caught yet.

There was a time when a fool and his money were soon parted. Now with the I.R.S. it happens to everybody.

Jack Carter says: "I took a 50% depreciation for myself on my taxes because my wife says I'm only half the man I used to be."

I've come to the conclusion that poor people in this country don't need a tax cut. They need to be made rich so they won't have to pay taxes.

Did I tell you about this man who deducted $5,000 because he had water in his basement? Then they found out he lived in a houseboat.

Some taxpayers do go a little too far. How about the character who was cheating with a doctor's wife and listed it on his income tax as medical expenses?

In America we have about 70 million taxpayers who are alive—and kicking. If you can pay your income tax you should count your blessings—because there is nothing else left.

I've saved the money to pay my income tax, now all I have to do is borrow some to live on . . . Everything I have I owe to the Internal Revenue.

The only problem about having an accountant to save you money by working on your tax returns is that their fees cost you more than they save you.

Nothing is certain but death and taxes, and each gets you in a hole . . . There's one consolation about life and taxes: when you're through with one, you're through with the other.

182

My neighbor protested an I.R.S. ruling that a baby born on January 15th was not deductible on last year's income. "Why not?" he asked, "it was last year's business!"

You may not know when you're well off, but the I.R.S. does . . . Four hundred years ago when the Indians were running this country, there were no taxes, no national debt, no foreign entanglements, and the women did all the work. What I don't understand is how the white man thought he could improve on a system like that.

People who squawk about their income taxes may be divided into two classes: men and women. This man stormed into the postmaster's office yelling, "I've been getting threatening letters in the mail for months and I want it stopped." The postmaster asked, "Sure, it's a federal offense. Do you know who's sending them?" He said, "Sure—it's those idiots at the Internal Revenue Service."

"How's business?" I asked my neighbor. He said, "Rotten—if it keeps up my income tax report will be just about correct."

Earning money would be a pleasure if it wasn't so taxing. Like the man who was filling out his income tax papers and cried, "Who says you can't be wounded by a blank?" . . . I know an introvert who was cured by an income tax inspector —he was keeping too much to himself.

Let's face it: A politician's idea of cutting corners is leaving on a government junket during the middle of the week, when the rates are cheaper!

I'm not taking any chances this year. I'm having my income tax return prepared by an expert: H and L Loophole! . . . H and L are great. If a mistake is made in the preparation of your tax returns, an H and L representative will be there to console you during each and every visitor's day . . . and they will help negotiate the sale of rights to your prison memoirs.

Interest rates are so high now and they're getting higher all the time. If Willie Sutton were around today he wouldn't have to rob banks—he'd open one . . .

Do you realize that every bank in town is charging at least 19% interest on its loans? And *you* didn't believe it when you heard organized crime was planning to take over legitimate, respectable businesses! . . .

A 19% interest rate is when you can truthfully say to your banker, "I'll be forever indebted to you! . . ." It just doesn't make sense. Why should I pay interest of 20 cents on the dollar to borrow a dollar that's worth only 20 cents? . . . Sure we've got runaway inflation. Sure, interest rates are soaring. But look on the bright side: the price of gasoline hasn't gone up since noon yesterday.

"My checking account balances perfectly," the young bride told her husband, "I'm overdrawn exactly what I'm short . . ." He started a joint account for the convenience of his new wife, but keeping the stubs in order was a little too much for her. He growled at her one night, "The bank has just returned your last check, dear." She clapped her hands joyfully. "Goodie—now I can buy something else with it."

You never know the real value of money until you try to borrow some . . . One woman wanted to arrange for the disposal of a $1,000 bond and phoned her bank. The clerk asked, "Madam, is the bond for redemption or conversion?" The woman said, "Well, am I talking to the First National Bank or the First Baptist Church?"

My bank is very careful. They send out their calendar one month at a time . . . I won't say my account is low, but my bank just sent me *last year's* calendar . . . I'm taking no chances on this economy. I'm putting all my savings in regular banks at 5% interest. That way no matter what happens over the years, if the stock market collapses, if inflation continues, if traditional investments fail, I know that in 10 years I'll be flat broke.

A series of eight forged checks turned up in the bank within a two-week period, all cashed by the same teller. The bank president asked her about it. "Why didn't you check his identification more closely?" She said logicaly, "Because he looked so familiar."

She explained to her friend, "But he's so much older than you, he won't enjoy the same things you do." She answered, "That's unimportant. I love Malcolm for what he is—president of the bank."

Everybody is always picking on poor bankers—and rightly so . . . After all, what is a banker?—A pawnbroker with a manicure . . . A banker is a fellow who lends you an umbrella when the sun is shining and wants it back the minute it begins to rain.

A bank is an institution where you can borrow money if you present sufficient evidence to show that you don't need it. "$50,000—that's a lot of money you want," the president of the bank said. "I'll have to have a statement from you." The applicant said, "Well, sir, and you may quote me—I'm very optimistic."

Why should anybody ever want to rob a bank? According to their advertising—it's easier to borrow all you want. The trouble is, the guy who writes the advertising is not the one who gives you the loan . . . The man screamed at the loan arranger: "Of course I don't have any security—that's why I want the money . . ."

Sign in the window of a local bank: "Loans for those who have everything—and haven't paid for it yet."

I got a friend who borrowed $10,000 and spent one year opening bank accounts. He got free radios, TV sets, luggage, clocks, pots, pans, dishes. At the end of the year he gave the ten grand back—and opened his own discount house . . .

A bank is a place you borrow money from when you can't get it from a friend . . . The furrier pleaded with his friend

185

at Chase: "I can't meet my note for $5,000 by next Monday—you'll have to give me an extension . . . By the way, were you ever in the fur business?" The Chase man said no. The furrier said, "Well, by Monday you will be."

My neighbor went to the bank and applied for a loan, and to his surprise he got it immediately. The next day he went to the bank and withdrew all the money he had on deposit there. He explained, "I don't trust a bank that would lend money to such a poor risk."

Old bankers never die—they just lose interest . . . I just can't figure banks out. They say, deal with a bank you can trust—trust is everything. You walk inside the bank, all the fountains pens are chained down.

A beautifully built Dolly Parton-type blonde wearing a tight sweater went into a midtown bank and put $6,000 in gold coins on the counter. The bank clerk winked and said, "Naughty girl, you've been hoarding, haven't you?" She snapped, "It's no business of yours how I got it—just deposit it in my account."

The banker was annoyed at the guy: "Your finances are in terrible shape—overdrawn accounts, extended loans—why do you allow your wife to spend more than you make?" He said, "Frankly, because I'd rather be bawled out by you than by her."

The unluckiest man in America practiced for five years forging another man's signature on checks. When he perfected the signature, signed a check and tried to cash it, the check came back marked "insufficient funds."

The holdup guy shoved the note at the bank teller which read: "I've got you covered, hand over all the dough in the cage." The teller handed him a note back: "Kindly go to the next window—I'm on my lunch hour."

It's not easy to win in business these days. If you do something wrong, you're fined—if you do something right, you're taxed . . . Success is making more money so you can pay off the taxes you wouldn't have to pay if you didn't have so much money already . . . My neighbor was glowing: "Business is wonderful—I never spent so much income tax in my life."

A business conference is a way to get other people to share your troubles . . . If you want to know how to run a big business, ask the man who hasn't any . . . The head of a large corporation was lunching with a group of his top executives, all of whom had unlimited expense accounts. When the check appeared, everyone grabbed for it, but the boss won. "I'll take it this time, boys," he said. "This time I can be sure I'll only pay for it once!"

Every boss knocks his employees and vice versa: "There must be some truth to the theory of reincarnation, the way some people come back to life at quitting time," one executive noted . . . One boss told the union delegate, "Quite a few people in this firm are already working a four-day week. The only trouble is that it takes them five days to do it."

The boss was evaluating the worth of one of his employees: "I'm overpaying him—but he's worth it." He approached the ambitious and competent young man and told him, "I've had my eye on you. You're a hard worker, and you've put in long hours. You're very ambitious." The employee smiled his thanks. "So, consequently," the boss added, "I'm going to fire you—it's men like you who start competing companies."

A manufacturer was reprimanding his son for being lazy. "Son," he said, "when I was your age, I worked sixteen hours a day learning the silk business . . ." "I'm very proud of you, father," replied the son. "If it hadn't been for your ambition and perseverance, I might have had to do something like that myself!"

The wife met her husband's 48-24-35 secretary for the first time: "I'm glad to meet you," she said. "My husband has told me so little about you . . ." One businessman who was supposed to marry his pretty model told her, "Darling, I'm ruined. My business has failed and I'll have to declare bankruptcy. I don't have a cent." The model replied, "Don't worry, sweetheart. I'll always love you, even if I never see you again."

The businessman was telling his wife the reason for the recession. He explained about the bank rates and the economic adjustment and inflation. "It's just wonderful," his wife said, "that anybody could know so much about money —and have so little of it."

Like the boss said to his departing executive: "In a way I'll be sorry to lose you. You've been like a son to me—insolent, surly, unappreciative . . ."

Everybody picks on bosses. The instructor at a company-sponsored first-aid course asked one of the union men, "What would you do if you found you had rabies?" He said, "Bite the boss . . ." "My boss is different," said my neighbor. "You just can't help liking him—'cause if you don't, he fires you!"

I wanted my son to share in the business," one big shot told me, "but the government beat me to it . . ." My neighbor confronted his doctor: "Remember you told me to go out with girls so I would get away from my business? Well, now will you help me get back my business?"

The glamour girl said to the male fellow worker: "Yes, I can tell you how I got my raise—but I don't think it will help you much."

This secretary kept making one terrible mistake after another. When he couldn't take it any longer, her boss finally lost his temper: "What the hell is the matter with you?" he screamed. "Are you in love or something?" She snapped, "I certainly am not—I'm a married woman."

The boss was basically a very softhearted man who wanted to help young people. After keeping this girl on for six months he called her into his office. "Sylvia," he started, "I'm going to give you an opportunity to make something of yourself—you're fired."

I do think we have gone too far with the automation bit . . . Man first makes the machine necessary and then the machine makes man unecessary . . . That's like building up your boarder to take your place at home . . . Everything is automated these days—yesterday I got an obscene phone call from a recording . . . To err is human: to really foul things up requires a computer.

The I.R.S. agent told the hysterical taxpayer: "We sympathize with your problems—but they can't fit into our computer . . ." Automation doesn't cut red tape—it perforates it.

Here's a very interesting item I picked up in the paper. It says that we will soon be able to buy an atomic-powered clock that will not lose or gain one second in three thousand years. Not only will it keep perfect time for three thousand years, but it also comes with a thirty-day guarantee.

Modern office machines have made clerical work 20 times faster now than in 1900. Not only that, it only takes three times the number of people to do it . . . I should be ashamed. You know what I did? I gave my record club a gift membership in my book club, and the book club a gift membership in the record club. The way I figure it, after billing each other for about three months, both computers will explode!

A man put a card in one of those date-matching computers that said, "I am young, handsome, and wealthy and I'm looking for someone to love." Out came a card from the machine: "Don't just stand there, kiss me! . . ." My friend was complaining that "they are really going a little wild with the automation thing—last year a computer went on my honeymoon . . ."

"I know, I know," the secretary said when she saw the new computer. "It's supposed to replace twelve men—but I'd rather have the men."

They had a tough day at the White House. The computer broke down and everybody had to learn to think all over again . . . This letter to a marriage-by-computer service: "I became a husband through your computer service. We have been happily married. I would, however, be interested in your new model."

My neighbor says: "It's odd. In the morning, I program my microwave oven to cook my dinner that evening; I've got an answering machine that lets me hear messages from people who called hours before; I've got a clock radio that I set at night to awaken me the next morning; and I've got a video tape recorder that records TV shows so I can watch them some other time. Suddenly I've got this weird feeling that my entire life is being postponed for presentation at some later date!"

Automation seems to be replacing men and women of all kinds—but it will never replace the taxpayer . . . There are so many labor-saving applicances on the market today that you have to work all your life to pay for them . . . My neighbor put it straight: "The machine that did away with the horse—is now doing away with me."

One factory put up this sign: "Look alive—you can be replaced by a button."

Automation has opened up for thousands of skilled employees a whole new world of unemployment . . . Starting next month, the post office will be charging extra postage for first-class mail that doesn't meet certain size limitations . . . You see, they're trying to automate the mail handling as much as possible, and if a letter is too big for the machine, then a postal employee will have to stop and take the time to mutilate it by hand!

When automation really takes over—we'll probably be working a no-hour week . . . Modern technology has given us so many substitues it's hard to remember what we needed in the first place . . . The technologists filled our homes with the future and left the repairs for today . . . The new

190

inventors do provide us with leisure time for reading, especially the yellow pages, under "Repairs."

Habitual dependence on automation can lead to softening of the brain. During the power failure many people complained of having gotten stuck for hours on escalators . . . One employee told his boss he was late because he got stuck on an escalator in the building. "Why didn't you just walk down?" the boss asked. He said, "But I was going up."

With the increasing respect for computerized judgment, we will soon accept the personality evaluation on weight-machine cards as character references.

It's not easy running a big business in the U.S. A new study indicates that, as a result of overwork, business executives are dropping like flies on the nation's golf courses.

One boss yelled at his assistant, "You're fired." He said, "Fired?—I thought slaves were sold . . ." It took the timid clerk three years to get up enough courage to ask for a raise. Finally one day he went to his boss and said, "Sir, for three years I've been doing three men's work for one man's pay. I deserve a raise." "I can't give you a raise," the boss told him. "But please give me the names of those two guys, and I'll fire them immediately."

The secretary answered the phone: "Our automatic answering device is away for repairs—this is a person speaking . . ." The executive called his secretary into his office. "Cindy, just because I make an occasional pass at you, and take you home once in a while, where did you get the idea that you could do as you damn please around the office? She said, "From my attorney."

Window sign in Abrams's clothing store: "Use our easy credit plan: 100 percent down—nothing to pay each month."

Martin went to Goldstein's Clothing Store to buy a new suit for a wedding . . ." You look like a real gentleman," said Goldstein. "Why don't you let me make you a special suit to order?" "I don't think so," said Martin. "Just tell me what kind of material you like. I'll write to England. They'll get the wool, then they'll weave the cloth, they'll ship it over. I make a pattern, you'll come in for two or three fittings and the suit'll be gorgeous." "But I need the suit in three days." "Don't worry! You'll have it!"

Two garment workers were sitting in a Seventh Avenue restaurant during the slack season. "Did you hear about Cooper?" one said. "His place burned down." The other said, "Glad to hear it. He's such a nice fellow—he deserves it."

New York is composed of little fiefdoms: Wall Street, the United Nations, the diamond center, Broadway. Today we'll take a laughing tour through Seventh Avenue—the garment center: I heard one manufacturer say, "Business is so bad that people are returning things they didn't even buy . . ." One salesman noted, "He's the toughest buyer I have to deal with. He not only demands tooth for a tooth, he expects yours to have gold in it."

One cloak and suiter was moaning, "I leave my problems at work—I have another set at home."

The bathing suit model just became engaged to the traveling salesman. "He's good-looking?" asked her friend . . ."Passable . . ." "He has maybe a good personality?" . . ."Fair . . ." "So, does he have money?" . . . "Nothing. . . ." "How about habits? He has any bad habits?" . . . "A little bit he drinks . . ." "So if there's nothing great about him, why are you marrying him?" She explained, "He's on the road all the time—who'll see him!"

These clothing manufacturers were on safari in Kenya. Deep in the heart of the Tsavo Game Park they came to a clearing in the bush. Irving froze. He whispered to his friend who was a few feet ahead of him: "Sol, don't turn around too quickly b-b-b-but is that a lion behind me?" "You're asking me?" replied Sol. "What am I, a fur salesman?"

The buyer told the cutter: "When Mr. Cohen's son starts working here tomorrow, he is to have no special privileges or authority. Treat him just as you would anyone else who is due to take over the business in a year or two."

A Myron Cohen classic is about the sportswear manufacturer who had gone bad and couldn't pay his bills. He decided to pretend to commit suicide and fake a funeral and his problems would be solved. At the bier the first creditor cried, "Poor Max. I'll miss him." "Yeah," sniffed the second creditor. "Too bad. Good old Max." But the third creditor was furious. "You bum, you louse," he snarled. "Pulling a fast one to get out of what you owe me." Even though you're dead I'm going to get personal satisfaction." With that he pulled out a gun and aimed. "Look, don't get excited," cried the corpse, sitting up, "*You* I'll pay."

The top salesman in "Junior Deb Frocks" won a two-week vacation in the Catskills. He oversexed himself and passed away. When his boss heard that happened, he cabled the hotel: "Arrange best funeral money can buy—but first send back his samples."

Max was explaining conditions in the garment center: "Business is like sex: when it's good, it's wonderful—when it's bad, it's still pretty good."

"I am not for women in business," one tycoon said. "If you treat them like men, they start crying and yelling—and if you treat them like women, your wife has got to find out about it."

This character was crying that business was so bad. "Last year alone," he complained, "I lost about 500 a week—week after week." His friend asked the logical question: "Then why don't you give up the business?" He answered just as logically, "Then how am I going to make a living?"

The businessmen were discussing a compatriot: "He used to work for me," said the first one. "I wouldn't trust him with

my money. He would lie, cheat, steal—everything for a buck."
"How do you know him so well?" "How? I taught him everything he knows!"

Automation is a $75-a-week clerk replaced by a $250,000
machine.

I figured out that it would take fifty people working day
and night for two hundred years to make the same mistake
an electronic computer can make in two seconds.

Don't misunderstand, I'm not really prejudiced against computers. But tell me the truth—would you want your daughter
to marry one?

I really believe they are going too far. There's a computer
now that is so human, when it breaks down they don't give it
oil—they give it Yuban coffee.

Mechanical things have always fascinated me. I guess I
inherited it from my grandfather who invented the burglar
alarm—Unfortunately, it was stolen from him.

Business is what—when you don't have any—you go out
of . . . What with parking difficulties, household errands,
and golf, it's almost impossible for a man to find any time for
his business.

Nobody makes house calls anymore. My car wouldn't start
so I called for a tow truck. The guy on the phone said,
"Sure—bring it in and we'll be happy to tow it for you."

Business was so quiet you could hear the overhead pile up—
so the boss had to fire his trusted employee. "The worst
thing about retirement," the man said, "is having to drink
coffee on your own time."

He was only getting $150 a week yet he had an automobile, a
yacht, country home, trips to Europe and all . . . His boss
became suspicious and asked, "I pay you only $150 a week,

so where are you getting the rest of the money for cars, yachts, traveling, etc.?" He said, "I earn over $2,000 by holding a raffle every week, selling tickets for only $1 apiece." "What do you raffle off every week?" "My $150-dollar-a-week salary."

Business worries kept him from sleeping at night and he was advised to count sheep when he got into bed. Next day he was asked if counting sheep put him to sleep. "No, I didn't sleep at all—the adding machine made too much noise."

The guy bragged endlessly about how his company had made him a vice-president until his wife got more than she could handle. "Look," she says, "there are vice-presidents falling out of every bush . . . Why, even over at the super-market they've got so many there's a vice-president in charge of peas." He couldn't let that one go. He called the super-market and asked for the vice-president in charge of peas. The guy on the phone said, "Canned or frozen?"

Meeting your expenses is easy—in fact, it's impossible to avoid them.

You can only fool some of the people some of the time—but that's enough to show a profit.

"That's right," the boss told his clerk. "I'm giving you a raise because I want your last week here to be a happy one."

If efficiency experts are so smart about running a business, how come they are always working for somebody else?

It's simple economics. America is the richest nation on earth because we own more Toyotas and Sonys.

There are still rich people around. My neighborhood is so rich, the high school mascot is a mink.

In Beverly Hills there's a rich school now called, "Our Lady of the Dow-Jones Averages."

My uncle is nearsighted and he's rich—that's why he has a prescription windshield.

Barbara Walters has it in her contract that she doesn't have to talk about any country that has less money than she does.

My wife found a way to save her money—she uses mine.

Inflation is when a supermarket holds a sale by rolling its prices back to 10 A.M.

Money isn't everything—you get the same results with a checkbook. Personally I don't like money—but it quiets my nerves.

I borrow all the money I can, and I don't worry about it. I figure by the time I pay it back, it won't be worth anything anyway. Economists are predicting that our standard of living will be higher in the 80s. We hope not—we can't afford what we have now.

I never get in the express line at a supermarket. Why should I be in a hurry to get robbed? Didja hear about the bandit who held up a supermarket while his wife was at the check-out counter? On his way out he tossed her the loot—and she was still $2 short!

Never mind rising medical costs—have you priced get-well cards lately? The real trouble with money is that you can't use it more than once.

"Well, I just worked out a budget and came to a decision," a harried man told his wife and children. "What?" the wife asked. The husband replied: "One of us will have to go!"

You can't take it with you because it goes before you do—I can't believe how expensive produce is now. The other day I went into a store to buy half a dozen tomatoes. I told the clerk all I had was a $10 bill. He said, "That's okay—you can pay me the rest tomorrow."

Someday I hope to be able to afford to spend as much as I do now.

It's called take-home pay because you'd be too embarrassed to take it any other place.

You can't take it with you when you go—but that's about the only place you can go without it.

Success is when you have your name in everything but the telephone directory . . . Success formula: Be nice to people until you make a million—after that, people will be nice to you.

This successful fellow dies and goes to heaven and when he arrives there's nobody there but the Lord and George Washington . . . And he says, "Where is everybody?" And the Lord says, "They're down below; open that door and you can see them." So he opens the door and a big band is playing, and they are swinging and dancing, and the fellow says, "Why is a big band playing down there and it's so quiet up here?" And the Lord says, "You don't think I'm going to book a big band for just two people."

Success story: ABC-TV has just announced that William F. Buckley has been signed to star in a 12-hour miniseries based on Webster's unabridged dictionary.

One of the most successful men in the business world attributes his millions to five things: Honesty, integrity, kindness, patience—and his uncle who died and left him millions.

The man was acting like a big success—putting on a big front. But he was behind in the payments on his new car. "Dear Sir," came one warning letter, "what would your neighbors think if we came and repossessed your car?" He replied, "Dear Sirs: I took the matter up with my neighbors and they all think it would be a very lousy trick."

It's a cinch to make money these days—it's just impossible to make a living.

The average man's biggest problem is that his paycheck comes minus tax and his bills come plus tax.

In 1625 Peter Minuit bought the island of Manhattan for $24—which is interesting only because one of his descendants last weekend paid more than that to park there.

Car sickness is what occurs when you see what the new models are costing.

Inflation is so bad, for the first time in history counterfeiters are going bankrupt.

The other day I went to have my battery replaced. When I got the bill, the mechanic listed $500 for labor. I said, "What do you mean $500 for labor?" He said, "Simple, my wife just had a baby."

The most important thing in the world is not money. It's love. I'm lucky. It just so happens, I love money.

So many people are on welfare in my old neighborhood, panhandlers are considered self-employed businessmen.

You've got to be smart to be in business today. I actually saw this sign on a closed Broadway store: "We undersold everybody."

I don't want to mention names, but I'll tell you how one dietician makes money. He puts his patients on a starvation diet and then asks them all for the cash they save on food.

Pretty soon a wheeler dealer in oil will be anyone who can afford to fill up his gas tank.

Inflation means that your money won't buy as much today as it did when you didn't have any.

My neighbor just figured it all out: "After they deduct from my paycheck the state, city, and federal income tax, social security, disability, and union dues—it costs me $16.25 just to report to work each week."

The way restaurant prices are going up—it won't be long until the hundred-dollar-a-plate dinner sounds reasonable.

Inflation is when you have to make twice as much money to keep up with your standard of living of last year—when you declared bankruptcy.

The only thing wrong with the dollar that used to buy three times as much is that we didn't have it then.

We may not be in a depression—but this is the worst boom we've ever had.

Last night I read a book that brought tears to my eyes—it was my bankbook.

I ordered a steak in one restaurant. The price was $18. I said to the waiter, "Are you kidding? How long are these prices going to last?" He said, "Only until tomorrow—the sale ends today."

Inflation means you never had it so good—or parted with it so fast.

Those advertising guys can sure make you believe it. I know one girl who is convinced her living bra bit her.

One minister I know believed very strongly in advertising and had a sign put up in front of his church which said: "If you are tired of sin—come in!" Some enterprising member of his congregation who also believed in advertising scrawled this additional message: "If you're not—call Buttermilk 5-8706."

It was this shoplifter's eighth offense at the same store. The president of the store finally had the thief brought to his office. "Let me ask you something," the president pleaded.

"Why is it my store you always pick to rob?" The thief said, "That's easy—you always advertise such terrific bargains."

The best things in life are free—no wonder they are never advertised . . . Advertising is usually a trick to get you to spend money, by telling you how much you can save . . . Here's a switch. I saw a commercial and a masseuse was squeezing Mr. Whipple . . .

Advertising can be very expensive—especially if your wife can read . . .

I asked one friend if advertising pays. He said, "Yes, indeed. Why only the other day we advertised for a night watchman and that very night the safe was robbed . . ." Richard Jacobs, the advertising genius of the Joseph Jacobs organization says, "Doing business without advertising is like winking in the dark at a pretty girl—you know what you're doing but nobody else does."

Some of those ads can be confusing if not amusing: One caterer's ad in the *Post* said: "*Are you getting married?—Or having an affair?*" . . . The ad for St. Paul Laundry says: "We do not tear your laundry with machinery—we do it by hand . . ."

I saw an ad for a loan company. It said: "Don't borrow from your friends—borrow from us . . . You'll lose your friends —you'll never lose us . . ." If advertising encourages people to live beyond their means—so does matrimony.

A serious ad in *Mines Magazine*: "Wanted: Man to work on Nuclear Fissionable Isotope Molecular Reactive Counters and Three-Phase Cyclotronic Uranium Photosynthesizers. No experience necessary."

A man lost a valuable dog and advertised in a newspaper, offering five thousand dollars for it, but got no replies. He called at the office. "I want to see the advertising manager," he said. "He's out," said the office boy. "Well, how about his assistant?" "He's out too, sir." "Then I'll see the editor." "He's out, sir." "You mean everybody is out?" "Yes—they're all looking for your dog."

Advertising costs me a lot of money—my wife keeps reading the ads.

The Joseph Jacobs advertising organization ran a series of ads for Hawaiian Punch that caused a little excitement. The ad showed a beautiful waitress serving a man a glass of Hawaiian Punch. The headline read: "He gets it downtown— why don't you give it to him at home?"

Outside the town of Comfort, Texas, which happens to be between the villages of Alice and Louise, a motel has this sign advertising: "*Sleep In Comfort Between Alice and Louise.*"

Real estate agents are mostly honest. You just have to know how to interpret their newspaper ads: "House for sale— charmingly rustic." This means the house has remained exactly as it was 50 years ago—when it was condemned. Or "Waterfront view"—whenever it rains, the backyard floods. Or "Surrounded by wildlife"—this will invariably be true— provided you think of mosquitoes as wildlife!

How about a little more truth in advertising? Just once I'd like to see a sponsor go on TV and say, "Our product is the same as it's always been for the last 25 years—only our price is new and increased."

Talk about progressive advertising: This department store ad in the *New York Post*: "Maternity dresses—for the modern miss."

Insurance is like sex—the older you get the more it costs . . . One saleman sold me group insurance—but the whole group must get sick before I can collect . . . My neighbor is in the insurance business. He sold me a 20-year-retirement policy. At the end of 20 years—*he* retires . . . My car has a fifty-dollar debatable policy.

She asked her insurance agent, "Should my husband die overnight, what would I get?" He said, "That depends on how the evidence is presented to the jury."

Insurance is the business of protecting you against everything, except the insurance agent . . . This insurance salesman had his prospect on the hook and was moving in for the kill: "That will only cost you $38.50 per month on a straight life," he purred. "Well," the prospect said sadly, "I would like to fool around once in a while on weekends."

It's a fact that this merchant bought fire insurance and the same day he had a fire and his store burned to the ground. When he filed his insurance claim, the company suspected arson but couldn't prove it. They wrote him this letter: "Dear Sir: You insured your store and contents against fire at 10:30 A.M. The official report indicated that the fire didn't break out until 4 P.M. the same day. Will you be good enough to explain the delay?"

The insurance man said, "Lady, you can't collect life insurance on your husband—he isn't dead yet." She said, "I know—but there's no life left in him."

Bob Hope is the richest of all the comedians and he is proudest of the fact that he carries more insurance than anybody. "I don't want to tell you how much insurance I carry with this company, but all I can say is—when I go—they go."

My neighbor told me: "After years of nagging, I finally bought one of those annuities but, of course, I didn't read the small print. Now I've discovered that to be eligible for compensation I have to be run down by a herd of wild animals on Fifth Avenue, then I collect $3 a week. If I lose my hair, the insurance company helps me look for it and they take marvelous care of my wife. They pay all maternity costs—after the age of 87."

A gentleman who had undergone a medical examination for a life insurance policy received a wire: "Regret to inform you that tests show you have pneumonia, heart disease, and ulcers." An hour later, however, a second telegram arrived. "Sorry," it said, "first telegram mistake. Confused your examination with that of another applicant." The relieved man wired them immediately: "Sorry, but I committed suicide half an hour ago."

The life insurance office was shocked by the 97-year-old man who wished to take out a policy. His application was turned down. Where upon the old gentleman said with annoyance, "You folks are making a big mistake. If you look over your statistics you'll find that mighty few men die after they're 97."

With all of today's attractive accident policies, a man can't afford to die a natural death.

Honesty is the best policy—unless you have general coverage in your insurance policy.

This man told the insurance company that his car was stolen and he wanted the money for a new car. The insurance adjuster told him, "We don't give you the money—we just replace your old car with a new one." He replied, "If that's the way you do business—you can cancel the policy on my wife."

The guy talks to his insurance man who is also a faith healer. "My uncle is very sick—I think you should know." The healer says, "Your uncle is not sick, he just thinks he's sick." Two weeks later he goes to collect the insurance and the faith healer asks, "How's your uncle?" And the guy says, "He thinks he's dead."

Life insurance is what keeps a man poor all his life so he can die rich.

A man never realizes the value of his home—until he has the occasion to collect the fire insurance.

The little boy was anxious to go in swimming but Mom said: "No—it's much too deep and cold." The kid said, "But Daddy is swimming." Mom said, "I know, dear—but he's insured."

The agent for the life insurance company paid the lady the amount of insurance her husband had carried. He then asked her to take out a policy on her own life. "That's a good idea," she said, "I think I will—my husband had such good luck with his."

He fell out of the window, feet first. His widow collected the insurance, as well as the Federal, state, and social security benefits. But then came the lawyers, relatives, government deductions, bills, inheritance tax, etc. When the doctor came to see her she was a wreck. "Sometimes," she cried, "I almost wish my husband hadn't fallen out of the window."

I've got a great health insurance policy. In case of illness or injury requiring hospitalization, they'll automatically provide me with a semiprivate bed . . . It's true they won't pay for a surgeon. But if I'm in need of an operation, they'll give me a butter knife and an easy-to read instruction booklet . . . So I bought a policy, and now I feel like I'm really in good hands—I just wish they weren't around my neck.

An insurance policy is an agreement made up of words that are too big to understand, and type that is too small to read . . .

An insurance salesman was getting nowhere in his attempts to sell a policy to a farmer. "Look at it this way," he said finally. "How would your wife carry on if you should die?" "Well," answered the farmer reasonably, "I don't reckon that's any concern o' mine so long as she behaves while I'm alive . . ." The salesman was pushing his policy: "I'll tell you why you should take out our accident policy. One month ago a lady took out a policy with us. Last week she broke her neck and we paid her $5,000—you may be the lucky one tomorrow."

A manufacturer who was considering joining a lodge asked the president of one of them, "Does your lodge have any death benefits?" "It certainly does," the lodge president replied. "When you die, you don't have to pay any more dues."

What really hurt Humpty Dumpty wasn't that he had a bad fall, but that he had recently let his accident insurance lapse.

Travel

When you start to look like your passport picture—you know you need a vacation.

"Good news! I've saved enough money for us to go to Europe," she said excitedly. "Wonderful," her husband said, "when do we leave?" She explained, "As soon as I've saved enough for us to come back."

I've traveled a little myself. I was in Rome and saw tourists throwing coins in that famous fountain. I threw in a check —at least it's deductible.

George Burns says: "Flying is more fun these days. At my age the biggest kick I get is being frisked at airports." On my last trip to Europe Sophia Loren was there and they frisked her for two hours—and she was seeing someone off.

This is the worst travel joke I ever told. It's about the couple who asked the travel agent to get them two tickets to the moon on the next flight out and to make reservations at the Moon-Hilton. "I'm sorry," said the agent, "they are not taking any more reservations—they have a full moon right now."

Everybody is going on cruises these days. There's one cruise you know you're going to have fun on. The highest ranking officer is the wine steward.

I was on a film festival at sea. It was rough. The sharks kept following the ship trying to break into show business.

The captain invited the beautiful young lady to his cabin. When she refused, he threatened to sink the ship with everybody on it. The next day she cabled her mom: "Having a wonderful time—real exciting—last night I saved the lives of 1,200 passengers."

As the ship was sinking, the captain lifted his voice to ask: "Does anybody know how to pray?" One man spoke up confidently: "I do, Captain." The Captain said, "That's fine— you go ahead and pray. The rest of us will put on life belts— they're one short."

The two men sat in their deck chairs and one asked the other for a cigarette. His friend gave him the cigarette commenting, "I thought you had quit smoking." The other replied, "I'm just at the first stage—I've quit buying."

The beautiful blonde was bothered by the character looking for a shipboard romance until she finally told him to desist. The wise guy snickered, "Oh, pardon me—I thought you were my mother." With that she smiled and purred, "It couldn't be—I'm married."

Tip to those going abroad: In an underdeveloped country— don't drink the water. In a developed country—don't breathe the air.

The tourist questioned the Tanzanian. "I hear that your water in this village is unsafe to drink. What do you do about it?" The native answered, "We boil it. Then we filter it. Then we put some chemical in it—and in the end, we drink beer."

I overheard a middle-aged couple saying to a travel agent: "We'd like a pleasure cruise—book us on different ships."

The New Yorker was driving through Arizona and was stopped by a motorcycle cop, who accused him of doing 85 miles an hour. "Eighty-five miles an hour?" he shouted, "That's silly—I haven't even been out an hour."

I asked my travel agent if it is still possible to see Europe on $5 a day. He said, "Sure—if your hobby is mugging."

Everybody can afford to fly today. One lady was telling the other girls in her organization about her great trip to Europe. "Did you go on a chartered flight?" one lady asked. She said no. One asked "Did you go on a group flight?" She said no. Another asked, "Was it an excursion rate?" Again she said no. Her friend said in exasperation, "You mean to tell me you traveled retail?"

Have you noticed that every year it costs less to fly to Europe and more to get to the airport?

Every year it takes less time to fly across the ocean—and longer to drive to work.

She bought a very cheap plane ticket to London. But she'll have to sit on Robert Morley's lap.

One thing is certain. The airlines care about you. One airline sent out letters to all the wives of businessmen who used the special half-rates, asking how they liked the trip. Thousands replied: "What trip?"

Bad weather made a number of flight delays at an international airport during one trip. I was growing increasingly impatient. When a further delay was announced I walked up to the ticket agent and said, "I don't see why you people bother publishing a flight schedule." He replied in his usual calm, professional tone, "Well, sir, we have to have something to base our delays on!"

Jackie Gleason says he won't fly because he has religion. He's a devout coward. He gets airsick when he licks an airmail stamp. His big complaint is, "How can you walk out on a bad movie?"

Those no-frills planes have got me crazy. I was on one plane so small I had to have the exact change to get on.

This one airline is so small they can't afford movies on the plane so they fly over drive-in theaters . . . On no-frill French airlines they don't show movies—they pass around French postcards.

The biggest scare I ever got in flying was when the pilot of my flight was in line ahead of me at the flight insurance counter.

I don't know if I care to try this airline again. Maybe you've heard of the company I flew with. It's called Kamikaze, Inc.

I'll tell you what really made me nervous. After we'd been in the air 15 minutes, the captain got up to go to the bathroom, and on the way, he got lost.

Those no-frills have so many different types of planes—you ride on everything but schedule.

Americans never believe they are having a good time on their vacations unless they are doing something they can't afford.

Last year on our vacation we stopped at a motel that had a big sign saying "Children Free"—They tried to give us two kids.

My neighbor told me: "We were behind schedule during our entire vacation trip. To begin with, we spent 3½ hours in the driveway, trying to fold up that stupid road map."

Have you seen the ads and travel books that tell you "See Europe on $5 a day." Actually you *can* see Europe on $5 a day—if you stay in a Russian labor camp.

Maybe you can't take it with you, but have you ever seen a car packed for a vacation trip?

The husband was telling the boys: "It's really a four-week vacation—I take two weeks and then my wife takes two weeks."

Traveling brings something into your life you never had before: POVERTY . . . In planning a vacation the rule is: take along half as much baggage and twice as much money. My neighbor told me: "We stayed home this year, we took a pay-later vacation *last* year."

All tourists are alike. They want to go places where there are no tourists . . . There were so many tourists on my last trip to Hong Kong, they were getting into each other's snapshots . . . A tourist is a person who travels thousands of miles to get a snapshot of himself standing beside his car.

The travel agents, airlines, and cruise ships are in a price war at the moment. My neighbor took me on one of those no-frill cruises—10 days and no nights . . . This travel agent said to the bargain customer: "For the price you have in mind, sir, I suggest you join the navy . . ." Mickey Freeman met a woman on a ship who said she lost her husband at sea. He said, "It must have been a terrible storm." She said, "No, he met a blonde on a Caribbean cruise . . ." One couple demanded of their travel agent, "Separate oceans, please."

Some tips on traveling: Those Europeans are pretty rich. Almost everyone drives a foreign car. I'll always think of Paris as a great big motel.

My neighbor just came back from his vacation abroad. "Did you see any signs of poverty over there?" I asked. He said, "Not only did I see signs of it—I brought some back with me . . ." A Europeon vacation is a great equalizer. People come back from them just as broke as their neighbors who couldn't afford to go.

My aunt signed up for one of those economy cruises: She stays home, but the company sends her picture postcards to mail . . My uncle sure beat the system. He took a "*Go now—pay later*" plan and didn't come back . . . If you didn't get to go away on a vacation this year, you can get the feeling by tipping every third person you see.

I love to travel. I've seen more strange places than a Swedish cameraman. But I'm always looking for something new. A travel agent described the lovely girls of Tahiti and I asked, "What's the best time to go there?" He said, "Between 21 and 45."

This man walked into a travel agency to buy a steamship ticket. "To where?" the agent asked. "Have you got a globe of the world?" The travel agent handed him a globe. The man turned the globe around and around looking at all the countries and continents. After 30 minutes he said, "Excuse me, don't you have anything else?"

My neighbor advises, "Travel is educational—it teaches you how to get rid of money in a hurry." I asked him where he was going this year. He said, "For my vacation, I'm going to the same place I went last year—to the bank for a loan."

The stewardess was complaining about her weekend at that resort hotel: "Those singles weekends are phony—instead of meeting a lot of single guys who want to get married, I met a lot of married guys who want to be single . . ." She did brag that she got a beautiful all-over tan on her vacation. "How did you get it?" I asked. She said, "I did everything under the sun."

My neighbor was telling me, "My wife deserves all the credit for stopping me from gambling away my salary—she spends it before I get it . . ." This year I sent my wife on a vacation to the Thousand Islands," he said, "and I told her to spend a week on each."

I was at a very exclusive hotel in Rio—even room service had an unlisted number . . . I was paying so much rent I decided to use all the facilities. I asked a native if there were any alligators in the water. He told me there weren't. I jumped in happily. After swimming a little way out the native hollered after me, "No alligators—the sharks scared 'em all away."

Kids

I'm not worried about what modern children know—I'm just worried how they found out . . . Children are a great comfort in your old age—and they help you reach it faster too . . . The little girl startled her parents when she asked: "Do you two have sexual relations?" Mother didn't show her horror as she answered, "Well, dear, of course we do." The kid asked, "Then how come I never meet any of them?"

One mother I know has a real problem. She has two daughters. One is mad at her because she won't let her wear a bra yet and the other is mad because she won't let her throw hers away.

Kids have it made today. Their mothers drive them everywhere: to school, to the movies, to dancing lessons, to their friends' homes. I know one kid who wanted to run away from home and his mother said, "Wait, I'll drive you." The teachers don't keep the kids after school these days. When 3:30 comes, they're afraid to be alone in the same building with them . . . The 10-year-old tripped as he left the classroom and banged his head on the door. "Now don't cry," said his teacher, "Big boys don't cry, do they?" The kid said, "Heck no—they sue."

The five-year old went with his mother to see a young couple's new baby. He gazed at the small, red, wrinkled face

219

for a long time . . . Then he said, "So that's why she had him under her coat so long."

Van Harris tells about the little boy complaining to his mother, "All the kids taunt me—they say I have a big head." And the loving mother consoled him: "Don't listen to them—they're jealous. You have a beautiful head. It's not big. Now dry your tears and run down to the grocery store and get me 25 pounds of potatoes." The little boy said, "Where's the shopping bag?" And his mother replied, "I haven't got one. Use your hat."

A Kentucky farmer was punishing his young son for pushing the privy out into the creek. "But gee whiz," said the boy, "Whatta you want to punish me for? After all, you asked me who did it and I told you the truth. When George Washington chopped down the cherry tree and told his father the truth, he didn't get punished." "That's so," said the farmer with a sly look on his face, "but when George cut down the cherry tree, his father wasn't sitting in it."

Kids rarely misquote you—especially when they repeat what you shouldn't have said . . . My neighbor reprimanded her son for using a four-letter word. The kid said, "But Mom, Redd Foxx and Buddy Hackett use that word all the time." Mom said, "So don't play with them no more."

My neighbor says, "My kids don't think they're having a good time unless they're doing something we can't afford."

America is a wonderful place—it's where the parents obey their children . . . I think the answer is simple. Parents should have a heart-to-heart talk with their children—they'll learn plenty.

Billy Graham arrived in a small town and asked a small boy where the post office was. When the boy had given directions, the evangelist said, "If you will come over to the Baptist church tonight, you can hear me give directions for getting to Heaven . . ." "I don't think I'll be there," said the boy. "After all, you don't even know your way to the post office."

The Sunday School teacher was describing how Lot's wife looked back and turned into a pillar of salt, when little Jimmy interrupted. "My mother looked back once while she was driving," he announced triumphantly, "and she turned into a telephone pole!"

When young David handed in a poor paper in his Hebrew class his rabbi reprimanded him: "I never saw so many errors. I can't understand how one person could have made all these mistakes." The kid answered, "One person didn't—my father helped me."

One little boy I know was pretty bad one day, so his father gave him a bit of a spanking and sent him to his room without supper: "And don't forget to say your prayers." The old man went to his room to see that the youngster did as he was told. The kid gave his usual blessings to his family, his friends, his teacher—everybody but his father. Then he turned to pop and said, "I suppose you noticed you wasn't in it."

The rabbi was telling his guests a story when his little girl interrupted, "Daddy, is that true—or is that preaching?"

Kids are really with it today. When I was a kid my parents told me about the birds and bees . . . Now little boys want to know about Dolly Parton and Raquel Welch . . .

I've been picking up a lot of tips from kids lately. Not about sex, this I can't use—but their jokes are good—these I can still use . . . Like the youngster who said, "Here is my report card, Daddy, and one of yours I found in the attic . . ." Or the boy who said to his gang, "I have to go now—If I'm not home by 10 P.M., my father rents out my room."

At one recess they were telling these: "Did you hear about the smart flea that saved up and bought his own dog?" . . . "Did I tell you about the absentminded cow who gave milk of amnesia . . ." "The baby owl who didn't give a hoot about anything . . ." "The person who was run over by a steamroller and was put in rooms 25 to 30."

Did I ever tell you about: "The person who kept both feet on the ground and had trouble getting his pants on . . ." "The sailor who got kicked out of the submarine service because he tried to sleep with the windows open . . ." "The guy who read a poster in the post office, 'Man wanted for robbery in New York' and applied for the job . . ." "Do you know why Robin Hood robbed only the rich?—because the poor had no money."

The father was hollering at his kid, "Always you ask me questions. What would have happened if I asked so many questions when I was a kid?" His son said, "Maybe you'd be able to answer some of mine."

The day the kid was confirmed, the old man decided to give him the today-you-are-a-man routine—he told him about the birds and the bees. Later, the young bar mitzvah boy told his friends, "You know the thing people do when they want babies? Well, birds and bees do the same thing."

Two truants were rapping. "Why don't you treat your old man with more respect," one asked. "I'm disappointed in him," he answered, "Mom tells me the stork brought me."

The peak years of mental activity are between four and 18— at four we know all the questions—at 18 we know all the answers.

One psychologist advises: "Slap your child every day. If you don't know why—he does." Dr. Joyce Brothers tells parents: "Don't give your kid his full allowance—keep some to bail him out."

My neighbor told me: "My kid ran away from home. If he hadn't—I would have."

Most kids are going steady these days before their voices do.

The hardest part of telling young people about the facts of life is finding something they don't already know.

We spend the first half of our lives trying to understand the older generation and the second half trying to understand the younger generation.

The generation gap is the difference between a ukulele and an electric guitar.

One teenager to another: "Now that your old man has given you a car, does he still give you a weekly allowance?" The other boy said no. So he asked, "How, then, do you pay for gas?" He answered, "Simple . . . when the tank is near empty, I let the old man drive it."

Child punishment American-style runs like this: The mother gets very dramatic and says to her kid, "Go to your room!" He's got a TV set there. He's got his own refrigerator; he's got a train set that goes through the other people's apartment and back again. They send his dinner in to him, leave him for the evening with an 18-year-old baby sitter—and he's being punished. His father didn't live like that on his honeymoon.

A teenager may not know how to raise children—but you can be sure she knows how to raise parents.

A teenager is an adolescent who is constantly irked by her disobedient parents.

The kid brought in a composition called "Our Cat." The teacher said, "This is the same thing your sister handed in last year." The kid said, "Why not? It's the same cat."

Most children reach the age of reason by the time parents lose theirs. The freshman's father made an unexpected visit to his son's fraternity house. It was about midnight when he rang the doorbell. "What do you want?" a voice rang out from the second floor. The father asked, "Does Harold Davis live here?" The voice answered, "Yeah—bring him in."

Today kids in school are allowed to use pocket calculators while taking a math test. When I was a kid I had to get the answers the old-fashioned way—from the smart kid next to me.

"Thank you, Daddy," the teenage girl exclaimed. "Gee, my very own phone—I feel so grown up." Pop smiled. "Here, take this envelope. This should make you feel even more grown up—your very own bill."

Kids today are no worse than they were 20 years ago—they just have better weapons. One teenager told her friend, "I hear the faculty is trying to stop necking in school." The other frowned, "Next thing you know, they'll be trying to make the students stop, too."

The teacher told the children in the class that she wanted them to write a composition that involved religion, history, and mystery. Some bright lad turned in this short one: "Holy Moses, the queen is pregnant. I wonder who did it?"

My neighbor read that in India it costs $350 to support one kid—so he sent his kid there.

My mother was a smart woman. Every time I'd take the cod-liver oil, she'd give me a dime for my piggy bank. Then when the piggy bank got full, she'd break it open and use the money to buy more cod-liver oil.

When I was a kid I walked five miles to school every day and five miles back, which was pretty stupid—the school was across the street from where I lived.

I grew up in a tough neighborhood. At my high school graduation, some kids received diplomas—others received suspended sentences. Once a week they held a mugging drill. When I was born I was issued a combination birth certificate and last will and testament.

That new Boy Scout group in the East Bronx is a pretty tough bunch. One kid received merit badges in camping, hunting, and shoplifting.

The only thing children wear out faster than shoes are parents and teachers.

Children are natural mimics—they act like their parents in spite of every attempt to teach them good manners.

My nephew said: "It's hard to explain to kids why a nation that spends billions for nuclear bombs is trying to outlaw firecrackers."

Out of the mouths of babes—comes poison ivy. The teacher was scolding the first grader: "When I was your age I could name all the presidents—and in the proper order." The kid answered, "Yes—but then there were only three or four of them."

"What are you doing home?" Mom asked. "I put a stick of dynamite under my teacher's desk." "You go right back to school and apologize." "What school?"

During a grammar lesson one day, the teacher wrote on the blackboard, "I didn't have no fun at the seashore." Then she turned to the class and said, "How should I correct this?" One kid hollered, "Get a boy friend."

I think it's ridiculous how some people spoil their children. Take my neighbor, for instance. His son has the only sandbox with reclining seats.

Uncle asked little Charlie, "How do you like school?" The kid answered, "Closed."

These days a high I.Q. child is a kid who says dirty words earlier than other kids.

Kids are always threatening their parents: "I'm gonna run away from home and I'm gonna run so far it'll cost you 14 dollars to send me a postcard."

Pity the poor teacher who has the worst kid on the block— but with a perfect attendance record. The teacher gave Tony a zero: "He doesn't deserve a zero—but it was the lowest mark I'm allowed to give."

The quality of education leaves something to be desired. Today when a kid gets a diploma from high school, somebody has to read it to him. "Mr. Gray," the professor asked, "what three words are used most among college students?" The student answered, "I don't know." The professor responded, "Correct."

According to a study, high school students do poorly on college entrance tests because they watch too much television. Most of them think Bunker Hill is where Archie and Edith live.

"My teen-aged daughter gave us a time last night," a weary office worker said. "She started to run away from home. Luckily, she never got beyond the front door." A concerned colleague asked, "What happened?" "The telephone rang," the father replied.

"Dear Mom and Dad," the college student wrote, "I haven't heard from you in almost a month. Please send me a check so I'll know everything is all right."

This kid was knocking his parents to his classmates. "I'll never trust my father again," he cried, "after the rotten, cheap, sneaking thing they did to me." He roommate asked, "What did he do?" He answered, "I asked him to send me $200 for a set of books—and he sent me the books."

My nephew is no dumbie. Sure, he flunked sex education last year—he also got to take it again this year.

When it comes to teenagers and automobiles, where they really need a stop sign is in the back seat.

I my neighborhood school, they had 54 dropouts within the first three weeks. That's right, 54 dropouts—and you know what? Fifty two of them were teachers.

My neighbor's son is improving—but his mother still goes to the P.T.A. meetings under an assumed name.

In the old days, if a youngster was in the principal's office, it meant the youngster was in trouble. Now it means the principal's in trouble.

The teacher lectured to her students on the subject of sex. "In moments of temptation," she said, "ask yourself one question—is an hour of pleasure worth a lifetime of shame?" One demure young lady in the back of the room spoke up and asked, "Tell me, teacher, how do you make it last an hour?"

The dean was the last speaker to talk on sex and was asked to make it brief. "Ladies and gentlemen," he said, "it gives me great pleasure"—and he sat down.

Remember the good old days when a student would write home: "Dear Pop, I got an A in engineering and business management. Send money for laundry." Now they say: "Flunked picketing—mail bail."

Sending a youngster through college these days is very edutional—it teaches parents how to do without a lot of things. My neighbor says: "My son in college is a firm believer in free speech. I believe him—that's why he always calls home collect." Kid said, "Listen Dad, I've come to the conclusion that it's time for me to stand on my own two feet—but I can't do it with my present allowance."

Parents spoil their kids: A teenage son of wealthy parents was having difficulty with reading and writing, but his mother appeared to be unconcerned. She told his teacher, "It really doesn't matter—he'll always have a secretary."

The kid brought home a terrible report card. "What the hell is this?" the old man asked. The kid explained: "You know how it is—things are always marked down after the holidays."

"Daddy," he asked, "why did you sign my report card with an "X" instead of your name?" "I didn't want your teacher to think that anyone with your marks had parents who can read and write."

With today's college kids, you never know if they're going to leave school with a diploma or a summons.

The kid was asked what he wanted for his birthday. He said, "I'd like a watch that tells time." His uncle asked, "Doesn't the watch you have tell time?" The kid said, "No—I have to look at it."

The child was being examined to test her reliability as a witness. "Do you know anything that is in the Bible?" the judge asked. "I know everything," she answered. "What?" the judge exclaimed in astonishment. "Tell us some of the things that are in there." She said, "Well, there's a picture of sister's boyfriend, one of my mother's recipes for creamed spinach, an old curl of mine, and the pawn ticket for daddy's gold watch."

My nephew is a nice kid, but he eats too slow. He had dinner the other night for 3½ hours. Who eats alphabet soup alphabetically?

What we need is a college to teach our children what they think they already know.

One college student was happy the summer was over so he could go back to school: "Education is a wonderful thing—if you couldn't sign your name, you'd have to pay cash."

Two young college kids were having a slight argument talking about their relationship. "I don't mind your mother living with us," the fellow was saying, "but I do wish she'd wait until we get married."

One father was complaining about his son. "I sent my son to college and he spent four years going to parties, having fun, necking, and carrying on. It's not that I'm sorry I sent him—I should have gone myself."

It was a pretty progressive school. Even the kid's father, one of the original playboys, was startled when he saw his kid's book on sex. He was reading to himself and then decided to talk it over with his son. He went looking for him and found him in a clinch with the maid. "Son," he said, "when you're finished with your homework, I'd like to talk to you."

Age

I found the secret of youth—I lie about my age.

When we talk about the good old days, we don't realize that the things that aren't what they used to be include us.

Nothing ages a woman faster than her birth certificate. Phyllis Diller says, "Thirty-five is a perfect age for a woman—especially if she happens to be 50." Phyllis says: "Don't worry about avoiding temptation as you grow older—it will avoid you first."

She even lies about her dog's age. She was telling a friend, "I may be past fifty, but every morning when I get up I feel like a twenty-year-old, but there is never one around."

Middle age is when work begins to be a lot less fun and fun begins to be a lot more work.

Japanese proverb: "When a woman subtracts years from her age, those years are never lost. They are merely added to the ages of her women friends."

He told her he wanted some old-fashioned loving—so she introduced him to her grandmother.

Young men want to be faithful and are not. Old men want to be faithless and cannot.

George Burns says: "Of course I'm against sin—I'm against anything I'm too old to enjoy."

I don't want to say George is getting old—but when he played the slot machine in Las Vegas—three prunes came up.

As far as I'm concerned, old age is always ten years older than I am.

You will always stay young if you live honestly, eat slowly, worship faithfully, and lie about your age.

Ask any woman her age and nine out of ten will guess wrong.

The elderly lady kept recounting all her ills to the doctor who couldn't care less: "What can I do, madam?" he put her down. "I have done all in my power—I can't make you young again, you know." She said, "I know that all too well—but I thought you might help me grow a little older."

An old man was being interviewed on television on his ninetieth birthday. "If you had your life to live over again, do you think you would make the same mistakes again?" The old man smiled. "I sure would, but I'd start a lot sooner."

Georgie Jessel just got a letter from an old-age home and it was marked "Urgent." Says Georgie: "If I knew I was going to live this long—I would have taken better care of myself." I said to Georgie, "I hope I look as good as you do when I'm your age." He said, "You did."

There are three ways you can tell when you're getting older. First is loss of memory—second and third I forget.

Sylvia was telling her friend Lucy, "My husband is so forgetful . . ." Lucy said, "So I've noticed; at the party last night I had to keep reminding him he's married to you and not to me . . ." I knew one guy so absentminded, he took his wife to dinner instead of his secretary.

My neighbor was telling me that his wife has the worst memory in the world. "You mean she forgets everything?" I asked. He said, "No—she remembers everything . . ." That Charlie is really getting absentminded. Last night he kissed a woman by mistake. "You mean he thought it was his wife?"—"I mean it *was* his wife."

This absentminded professor dictated to his dog and then tried to give his stenographer a bath . . . or the absent-minded girl fiddler who kissed her violin good-night and took her beau to bed with her . . . or the absentminded idiot who stopped his girl and went too far with his car.

How absentminded can you get? This guy parked his car in front of the loan company . . . or the waitress who kissed her boyfriend good night and then said, "Is that all, sir?" Or the guy who mislaid his umbrella and went from store to store to find it. When he found it he was jubilant: "You are the only honest shopkeeper in town," he told the owner, "all the others denied having it."

The man was lying in the gutter in his pajamas. He explained to the cop, "As far as I can remember it, my wife and I were sleeping in bed when there was a knock on the door. My wife said, 'Good heavens—it's my husband!' And the first thing you know—I jumped out the window."

The judge asked the defendant, "You mean to say that you threw your wife out of the second-story window through forgetfulness?" The man said, "Yes, sir—we used to live on the ground floor and I just forgot we moved."

He wasn't a professor, but he sure was absentminded. "Lady," he screamed at the pretty thing next to him, "what are you doing in my bed?" She said, "Well, I like this bed, I like this room, and I like the way you make love—and anyway, I'm your wife."

There are currently 35 books that tell you how to get along after you retire. What we really need is one that can tell you

what to do *before* . . . The old say, "I remember when . . ."
The young say, "What's new? . . ." Asked why he was going
to marry a glamour girl instead of some woman his own age,
grandpa said, "I'd rather smell perfume than liniment."

A new medical study claims the key to reaching old age is
sex and work—unfortunately, in old age sex *is* work . . . "I
can still do anything I could ever do," George Burns told me.
"Now it just takes longer to recover."

Women hate to admit there is such a thing as age . . . Phyllis
Diller notes, "Old age is when you stop wanting to be pretty
and settle for fascinating . . ." One wife said to her husband,
"I don't think I look 35, do you?" He said, "No I don't—but
you used to . . ." My aunt was asked by the magistrate,
"What is your age?" He cautioned, "Remember, you're under
oath." She said, "Twenty-one years and some months." The
judge asked, "How many months?" She said, "One hundred
and twenty."

The irony of life is that by the time you have money to burn,
the fire has gone out . . . This man was so old his social
security number is printed in Roman numerals—even his
fingernails are wrinkled. He was accosted in the village by a
stranger who said, "I beg your pardon, you sure look like
you've been around—how old are you?" He said, "I'm getting
on for 96." The man asked, "And you lived here all your
life?" He said, "Not yet."

The irony of life is that by the time you're old enough to
know your way around—you are not going anywhere . . .
The reporter was interviewing the old man on his 100th
birthday. "What do you think of modern day women?" the
young fellow asked. "I can't help you with that question,"
the old man said, "because I quit thinking about women
nearly three years ago."

The tourist with a camera around his neck had stopped
beside a tumble-down shack on a mountain road. Sitting on
the porch in a rocking chair was the perfect picture of a
rugged old mountaineer . . . "May I take your picture?" the

tourist asked . . . "All right with me," the man said. "Go ahead . . ." After he had made two or three exposures, the tourist said, "I've always wondered how you mountain people live to such a ripe old age. What is your secret?" . . . "No secret how I live," he said, "Everybody around here knows. I drink a quart of home-made whiskey every day, smoke half a dozen cigars that I make myself from my own home-grown tobacco, and I chase after all the neighborhood gals . . ." "That seems like a rather strenuous life for a man of your age," the tourist said. "Just how old are you anyway?" . . . "I'll be 32, come October," the man said.

Several women were chatting at a bridge party. One, who was suspected of being much older than she claimed, said with a sad face, "My, I hate to think of life at 40 . . ." One of her friends couldn't miss the opportunity to say, "What happened to you then?"

Two hundred and fifty years worth of actors, George Burns, Art Carney, and Lee Strasberg, made a picture called *Going in Style*. Burns told me, "We're at a funny age now; the other night Art, Lee, and I went to a porno movie—and fell asleep . . ." Art Carney says, "We're getting more theatrical engagements in our 80s—it's like the government's help for the elderly—they guarantee a steak when your teeth are gone."

The 80-year-old Strasberg says, "Kids say everybody has their own bag—I'm at the age now when my bag is a hot water bottle . . ." Art Carney says, "You know you've reached middle age when weight lifting consists of just standing up."

One distinguished old actor was telling his grandson about his fiancée, who is 18 years old. "Eighteen," the young man repeated incredulously. "How can you consider marrying a girl of 18!" Grandpa asked calmly, "Why not? She's exactly the same age as my first wife when I married her."

The patent-medicine quack was really throwing it: "Look at me," he said to his audience. "I'm 300 years old, hale and hearty—all from taking this miracle potion." One skeptical lady asked the faker's youthful assistant, "Is he really that old?" The lad said, "Lady, you'll have to ask somebody else—I've only worked for him for 100 years."

You're getting old when . . . you go off your diet . . . When the men in the office treat you like one of the boys . . . When the highlight of your senior citizens' Halloween party is "Bobbing for dentures . . ." Nothing can spoil a class reunion like running into a guy who married your old girl, has all his hair, and has gotten rich at the same time.

Stanley was pushing 70 and the doctor wasn't too pleased with his condition. "I'll have to be candid with you," he said. "You're getting on and if you want to live out your life in reasonable health, no more smoking and drinking for you— and you'll have to give up half your sex life." Stanley said, "Okay, doc, as you say! But which half do I give up—the thinking or the talking?"

Bert Parks was fired from "Miss America" because he's too old. Bert claims, "There isn't a single thing that I could do at 18 that I can't do now—which gives you an idea how pathetic I was at 18."

He's too old at 65? For what? He's supposed to introduce them—not make love to them. Anyway, for him that would be a memory course . . . George Burns is 85 and he's still going strong on TV, the screen, and on stage.

The girls want Bert Parks back because he treated them all like ladies . . . I was talking to one raving beauty (a raving beauty is one who came out last in a beauty contest) and she said, "He's there for entertainment, not breeding purposes."

One fan wrote to Bert and said, "I've watched you on TV for years and I love you. What do you need those creeps for— you belong in pictures. Hollywood is looking for new faces— why don't you send yours in?"

Bert Parks was more then an m.c. for "Miss America," he was the girls' adviser on all things romantic. One girl asked if sex is good. He explained, "It sure is—you can take it on a trip and you don't need batteries."

On his program Bert asked his beauty contestants what kind of man they'd prefer being shipwrecked with on a desert island. "I'd want a fellow who was a wonderful conversationalist," said Miss Chicago. "I'd rather have a guy who knew how to hunt and cook," offered Miss California. Miss New York said, "I'd settle for a good obstetrician."

One pretty thing from Georgia was telling Bert about her wild night with a local lover boy. "Do you tell your mother everything?" Bert asked. She volunteered, "Certainly not. My mother couldn't care less—it's my husband who's so damn inquisitive.

Middle age is when it takes longer to rest than to get tired.

Georgie Jessel is approaching middle age for the third time. Georgie claims there is only one difference between himself and Burt Reynolds. "We're both popular," he explains, "but when my fans swoon it takes them longer to get up."

Religion

A little girl's prayer: "Please, God, make the bad people good—and the good people nice." Youngsters are proving that religion is coming back. Even Dial-A-Prayer put on three extra numbers . . . One kid asked his minister for something. He wouldn't give it to him, so he went over his head and prayed.

"Do you say your prayers before eating?" the teacher asked the 7-year-old. "It ain't necessary," she answered, "my mom is a good cook."

"And now, children, who can tell me what we must do before we can expect forgiveness of sin?" the teacher asked. "Well," said little Johnny, "first, we've got to sin."

The pretty little girl was making her first appearance in church. "How did you like it?" the preacher asked after the service. "Well," she answered, "the music was nice—but the commercials was too long."

The six-year-old was sent up to bed after dinner. "Say good night to all our guests," her mom told her, "and don't forget to say your prayers." "Okay," said the child. "Anybody need anything?"

There are so many headaches in the world today—if Moses would come down from Mount Sinai now, the tablets he would carry would be aspirin . . . The world is full of two kinds of people. The givers and the takers. The takers eat well but the givers sleep well.

One six-year-old boy was reprimanded by his Sunday School teacher: "You've been nothing but trouble—you're just a rotten kid." The little boy pulled himself up to his 3-foot-nothing and answered, "That's not true. I am so a good boy—God made me and he don't make no junk."

Like I've been telling you, it's more blessed to give than to receive, and besides, you don't have to write thank-you notes . . . An optimist is a man who goes to the window in the morning and says, "Good morning, God!" A pessimist says, "Good God—morning!"

This lady wanted to mail a Bible to her son at college. The post office clerk wanted to know if the package contained anything breakable. She said, "Only the Ten Commandments."

One day the telephone rang in the office of the pastor of ex-President Carter's Washington church, and an eager voice said, "Tell me, do you expect the President to be in church next Sunday?" "That's something I cannot promise," the minister explained patiently. "But we expect God to be here, and we think that will be incentive enough for a reasonably large attendance."

All the trouble started in the Garden of Eden when Eve bit into a piece of fruit. It was nothing compared to the trouble Jimmy Carter had when he did the same thing in Mexico.

Religion is making a big comeback. The *Reader's Digest* is coming out with a condensed version of the Bible so that it can reach everybody in a hurry . . . When they say condensed, they mean condensed. From what I understand, the new version will tell the story about how Moses spent two weeks wandering in the desert . . . And their special feature will be "My most unforgettable character," by Adam!—The suspense is killing me. Who's it gonna be—Eve or the snake?

244

There are about 10 million laws on the books, all trying to enforce the Ten Commandments . . . Come to think of it, if everybody obeyed the Ten Commandments there would be no Eleven O'Clock News . . . Sam Levenson reminds us that "Different people look for different things in the Ten Commandments. Some are looking for divine guidance, some for a code of living, but most people are looking for loopholes."

A nice but blundering old lady liked the new pastor and wanted to compliment him as she was leaving church after services. So she said to him, "I must say, sir, that we folks didn't know what sin was until you took charge of our parish."

When the old man came to see his son in America, he was shocked to find that the young man did not follow the orthodox laws. "You mean," he said, "you don't keep the dietary laws?" "Papa, I eat in restaurants, and it's not easy to keep kosher." "Do you keep the Sabbath, at least?" "Sorry, papa, it's tough in America to do that." "Tell me, son," the old man sneered, "are you still circumcised?"

Some instant versions of the Bible: "The leopard shall lie down with the kid—but every morning they'll have to come up with a fresh kid . . ." "Lead us not into temptation. Just tell us where it is—we'll find it . . ." "You must pay for your sins. If you've already paid—please ignore this notice . . ." There are so many new versions of the Bible but people still sin the same old ways.

"I was praying that the rich should give more money to the poor," the rabbi was telling his wife. "Do you think your prayers will be answered?" the wife asked. "Well, at least half of it is already answered; the poor will accept the money."

Now that there's no more praying allowed in school, the kids may have to go to motels just to read a Bible.

The preacher was telling his class that there are over seven hundred different kinds of sin. The next day he was besieged with mail and phone calls from people who wanted the list—to make sure they weren't missing anything.

"We have a lot of good religious people here," Bob Hope says. "I'm the first to tell you my wife is a good Catholic. We can't get insurance—too many candles in the house . . . Do you know our grocery bills are astronomical? Three thousand a week—fifty for food and the rest for candles."

I never refuse to do a Catholic benefit. I did once. Cardinal Cooke asked me and it snowed in my living room for three days—in Miami—during the summer . . . I did a Catholic benefit last night. I know it was a Catholic benefit because I left my car in front of the hotel and they raffled it off.

I am passing on some of the greatest one-liners since the Ten Commandments: Alan King: "Anyway, the priests so far have the lowest divorce rate . . ." Billy Graham: "A Christian should so live that he would not be afraid to sell the family parrot to the town gossip."

A young clergyman, fresh out of the seminary, thought it would help him in his career if he first took a job as a policeman for several months. He passed the physical examination and then took the oral examination to ascertain his alertness of mind and his ability to act quickly and wisely in an emergency. Among other questions he was asked, "What would you do to disperse a frenzied crowd?" He thought a moment and then said, "I would take up a collection."

One little boy was given a spanking by his father for messing up the house. He ran to his mother crying, "Mommie, you should have married the Pope—he loves little children."

His Holiness told one little girl to pray in private and she would be rewarded publicly. She was on her knees before going to bed when her father came in and asked what she was doing. "I'm praying," she anwered. "But I can't hear you," he said. She answered, "I wasn't talking to you."

246

Any man of religion will tell you that a dose of joy is a spiritual cure: Danny Thomas asks, "Do you think the Three Wise Men are the guys who got out of the stock market at the right time?" . . . Bob Hope wants to know, "Would you say a monastery is a home for unwed fathers?" . . . Steve Martin notes, "Union officials have only one thing against God—he worked a six-day week."

The farmer came up to the evangelist and told him he had "got religion" . . . "That's fine," said the preacher, "but are you sure you are going to put aside all sin?" . . . "Yes, sir," said the farmer, "I am through with sin" . . . "And are you going to pay up all your debts?" asked the preacher . . . "Now, wait a minute, preacher," said the farmer, "you ain't talking religion now, you're talking business."

Father Bob was having dinner at Danny's with Rabbi Mann. "Come on," said Father Bob, "when are you gonna let yourself go and have some bacon or ham?" "At your wedding," said the rabbi.

"I don't know if God exists," said one university professor, "but with what's going on in our colleges today, it would be better for His reputation if He didn't."

Ethnic Humor

The editor of the *London Times* received a letter from Edinburgh which stated, "If you print any more jokes about Scotsmen being frugal, I shall stop borrowing your paper."

Earl Wilson invented Ethnickia. Which proves that no shape, size, or shade has a corner on dumb-dumbs. I know a guy who made a fortune. He bought a thousand garbage trucks and sold them to the Ethnickian people as condominiums with escalators.

This Ethnickain is so honest that he worked in a Turkish bath for two years—and never took a bath.

Do you know what the city does when an Ethnickian fails to pay his garbage assessment? They stop delivery.

Did you hear about the Ethnickian scientist who developed an artificial appendix?

This Ethnickian went hunting and when he was deep in the forest he came upon a nude girl. "Are you game?" he asked. She said yes—so he shot her.

Ethnic humor is the sincerest form of flattening—especially in the hands of a bigot. Introduce an Italian as "The man who did so much for our country—but did he have to do it in my neighborhood?" and they take the racist out with laugh cramps . . . The fact is, the same joke can be applied to any nationality or creed. No race, creed, or color has the corner on dumb-dumbs: Like the two Jewish astronauts are talking, "What's the big deal about going to the moon? We're Jews, we go direct to the sun." The other astronaut said, "But if we get within 12 million miles of the sun, we'll melt." And the first one answers, "So what—we'll go at night!" Certainly this joke can be applied to two Germans, Irish, or black astronauts, or any two smart astronauts.

Down through the years the ethnic joke has been aimed at "this year's target." The joke about "How can you tell the bride at a Jewish wedding?" "She's the one with the price tag still on her gown . . ." later became "How do you tell the bride at a Puerto Rican wedding?" "She's wearing something old, something new, something borrowed, something blue, something yellow, something pink, something red . . ." Later it became, "The Irish bride?"—"She's the one in the maternity dress," or "The Polish Bride?"—"She's the one wearing the clean bowling shirt."

They're funny only if you remember that they are caricatures of the minorities—and they can apply to any minority. Like the friends who are telling stories and one says, "Did you hear about the two Jews who got off a bus and—" One guest interrupted and scolded, "Why are you always picking on Jews—can't you talk about the Greeks or Germans or Japanese for a change?" The guy said, "Sure, I'm sorry. Did you hear about the two Japanese gentlemen who got off a bus and one said, 'Are you coming to my son's bar mitzvah Saturday?'"

I'm not taking chances, I'll call them ethnic and you fill in your own dumb-dumb . . . and I'll . . . write . . . slowly . . . . because . . . I . . . know . . . they . . . can't . . . read . . . too . . . fast: Did I tell you about the ethnic in the army who didn't want the enemy to know he was out of ammunition—so he kept firing? . . . This ethnic claims that his grand-father was the man who invented the mule and put thousands of people out of work . . .

My ethnic friend told me, "I almost drowned yesterday. It taught me one thing—never take acupuncture treatments on a water bed."

Do you know what the ethnic lady does with her birth control pills?—She feeds them to storks.

Did I ever tell you about the ethnic vampire who bit Dolly Parton on the neck?

Did Earl Wilson tell you about the Ethnickian girl who told her mother she was expecting. Her mother said, "Are you sure it's yours?" . . .

My secretary walked into this coffee shop with a thermos and asked the man: "How many cups of coffee do you think this thermos will hold?" He said, "About five." She said, "Good—give me two black, two light, and one no sugar."

Charlie and Irving were told to paint the flagpole. Charlie stood on Irving's shoulder and reached as far as he could. The boss passed by and asked what they were doing. "We got to measure how high it is so we can figure out how much paint we'll need." The super said, "That's silly—take the flagpole down and lay it on the ground if you want to measure it." Irving said, "A lot you know. We want to find out how high it is—not how long it is."

Mr. Dumb-dumb was pacing up and down the maternity ward when the nurse finally came out and gleefully announced, "Congratulations—twins." He said, "Please don't tell my wife—I want to surprise her."

The busy executive was having trouble with his electric bills. Every month, after he had mailed his check, he was notified that he had sent the wrong amount. After several months of this endless disagreement—further confused by the company computer—a kindly soul at the electric company penned a note to the man: "Please pay the amount. You have been paying the date."

I saw a great black vaudeville show at the Village Gate called *One Mo' Time*. Black (is beautiful) humor and I expect to go back at least "one mo' time" to listen to them revive the old black classics. Like Bert Williams's line: "If you have two wives, that's bigamy—if you have many wives, that's polygamy. If you have one wife, that's monotony."

Bill "Bojangles" Robinson loved to tell the story of the black lady who has a man arrested for rape. They are both in court and the judge asks when the rape took place. "Yo honor," says the lady, "I don't exactly remember, but it seems to me it was just rape, rape, rape—all June, July and August."

Bojangles made audiences scream with the tale of the little black soldier who tried to leave camp and was stopped by the sergeant. "Where you going?"—"Out."—"No you ain't."—"Yes ah iz."—"You ain't goin' no place," said the sergeant. "Look," said the soldier, "I got a mother in heaven, a father in hell, and a girl friend in Harlem—and I'm gonna see one of 'em tonight."

The put-down has been the black comic's trick to answer his hecklers: Sam Burns, a southern Negro, was refused entrance in a "white" church. The sexton told him to go to his own church and pray to God and he will feel much better. The next Sunday he was back again. "Don't get upset," he said to the sexton. "I'm not forcing my way in. I came to tell you I took your advice. I prayed to God and he told me, 'Don't feel bad about it, Sam. I've been trying to get into that church myself for 20 years and haven't made it yet."

Sammy Davis, Jr. tells the story of the handsome black lad who goes to heaven and Saint Peter stops him at the gate: "This is only for heroes." The boy says, "You're looking at the greatest hero of all time." Saint Peter said, "What heroic thing did you ever do?" He said, "I was married to a white girl on the steps of Biloxi, Mississippi, City Hall at twelve noon." Saint Peter asks, "When did this happen?" . . . "Two minutes ago."

Bert Williams was the first of the great black comedians. His favorite story was about the man who is brought before the judge for stealing a chicken. The judge couldn't understand how a man could steal chickens with dogs in the yard. "No use to explainin' to you, judge," the old Negro answered. "If you tried it you would get eaten up or shot full of buckshot—and get no chicken either. If you want to engage in any rascality, judge, you bettah stick to duh bench what you am familiar."

Redd Foxx: "When I was in the service, there was one battle I'll never forget. I backed up so far I bumped into a general. He said, 'Why are you running?' I said, 'I'm running because I can't fly . . .'" Dick Gregory says he never will forget his first physical exam. The sergeant asked, "What were you in civilian life?" and Dick answered, "Deliriously happy."

John Wayne said he defeated so many Indians in the movies—he got hate mail from Marlon Brando.

A tourist driving through Arizona was stopped by an Indian selling blankets. "How much?" he asked. "Fifty dollars," said the Indian. "I'll give you ten," said the tourist. "Oh no, brother—no more deals like Manhattan."

One bar in New York hired an Indian as a bartender and had to fire him five minutes later. One customer ordered a manhattan and the Indian charged him 24 dollars.

I wasn't there, but they say it's a true story. When Columbus landed, a couple of Indians watched as they unloaded the cargo. Chris himself approached the two redskins. "*Buenos dias,*" he greeted them. One Indian turned to the other and said, "There goes the whole neighborhood."

With all the juvenile delinquency, inflation, crime, Watergate, bombings, and uprisings going on—I think maybe the Indians should have had some stricter immigration laws.

Did you hear about the Indian hypochondriac who switched to filtered smoke signals?

Listen, I've seen so many lousy westerns on TV—I think I hate those cowboys more than the Indians do.

Tonto and the Lone Ranger were surrounded by Indians when the Lone Ranger turned to Tonto and said: "We're in trouble, Tonto." To which Tonto replied, "You mean you're in trouble, white man."

The Indian out West was leaning against the post. The tourist disturbed him. "Why don't you get a job and invest your salary, make money—and then you won't have to work any more?" The Indian grunted, "Why go through all that? I'm not working now."

You can lead an Irishman to water, but you can't make him drink it . . . "Dump a few more cherries in my old-fashioned," Clancey told the bartender, "my doctor keeps telling me to eat more fruit . . ." Pat told me, "I've learned how to cut my drinking in half. Every day before I got to Murphy's saloon it drink five glasses of water—that takes care of the chasers right there!"

McGinty marched up Fifth Avenue in the St. Patrick's Day parade. He forgot to make a left turn and wound up in the East River . . . it was the only water he touched all day.

Billy Carter is a light drinker—as soon as it's light he starts drinking . . . Billy was told by his doctor that if he gave up whiskey it would lengthen his days. "You're so right," said Billy. "I recall one day I didn't drink at all and I never went through such a long day in my life."

The long-suffering Irish housewife went to see a marriage counselor and told how her husband Pat was a drunk, a bully, and an idler.

"If he's as bad as all that," the wise man said, "why on earth did you have seventeen children by him."
"I was hoping to lose him in the crowd," the lady replied.

The Irish are always fighting among themselves—to be sure of having worthy adversaries. The famous Irish author George Moore was asked on his 80th birthday to explain how he managed such a long life. "Easy" he said. "I believe it's due to the fact that I never smoked, drank, or touched a girl until I was 10 years old."

The Irish drink harder and fight harder than any people on earth—no wonder they call them the Jolly Green Giants. Clancy was complaining about "those darn scientists." Pat asked, "You mean about going to the moon?" He said, "No— those idiots fooled around 'till they came up with something besides whiskey to cure a cold."

New York City, etc.

George M. Cohan said it: "Living outside of New York is like living in a tent—to a New Yorker, anyplace outside of New York is Bridgeport."

Now that Mayor Koch's pooper-scooper law is working—yesterday I saw a St. Bernard with a roll of Charmin around his neck—he is on a Keep New York Beautiful kick: "Plant flowers in a pothole." He is putting up signs all over Manhattan: "Keep New York clean—take your trash to New Jersey."

God created heaven and earth in six days and New York is still unfinished—The Indians had the right idea. They got rid of Manhattan before they had to pay taxes on it.

In New York, the City Council is considering a proposal to make marathon running illegal. They claim it gives the city a bad image—the runners keep beating the New York City buses.

You ever ride on the buses? Those buses are so bumpy you can jog to work sitting down.

One girl on Eighth Avenue put it this way: "Sex is here to stay, and inflation is here to stay—so get it now while you can afford it." One local massage parlor on 8th Avenue asked the Mayor for a license to hold a sidewalk sale.

New York panhandlers really have chutzpah. I was walking up Madison Avenue with my gorgeous wife when a character asked me for $5. I was in a good mood and I gave it to him. Then he asked my wife if she'd join him for a drink.

I love New York. Like the song says, "It's a helluva town." George M. Cohan said it: "Anyplace you go outside of New York, you're slumming . . ."

Mayor Koch is doing a fabulous job. He found out how much money they made at Aqueduct Race Track last year—now he wants to take out the City Council and put in horses . . . New York is one city where you can get away with murder—unless you're parked beside a fireplug . . . One councilman came up with a solution for elementary traffic and parking problems in New York: "Encourage car thefts."

The crime situation is looking up. Some of the muggers are now giving green stamps . . . A new public opinion poll was released today. The question was, "Do you think there is too much crime in New York City?" 62% said yes, 23% said no, and the other 15% tried to mug the guy who was taking the poll . . . My uncle Charlie has just completed his new book entitled, "1001 things you can get for free in New York and where to steal them."

I admit we are all suffering from the hardening of the traffic arteries . . . Jerry Lewis says, "The last time I went to New York it was incredible. We circled the airport for hours. What made it incredible is, we were in a bus . . ." Jan Murray says that the traffic in New York is so bad, rescue planes had to drop supplies to the Good Humor man . . . Milton Berle says, "The best way to kill an hour in New York City is to drive around the block . . ." Forget the drive-in theaters—what we need are drive-in streets.

I love our sanitationmen. They are so considerate. They always leave you a little to start again with . . . Out-of-towners think New York streets are paved with gold—it must be a shock to them to see they're not paved at all . . .

Bob Hope reminded me that New York is a great town for sailors: "Last night I saw a lot of navy men looking for culture on 42nd Street—the only place you have to be vaccinated to go to the movies . . ." As Bob always says, "Love thy neighbor—but draw the blinds first."

I have a special announcement for all pedestrians in New York City. It has been estimated that by the year 2000, there will be twenty million cars in New York City, so, anybody wishing to cross the streets should do so at once.

On one crowded bus, the man asked the lady politely, "Madam, would you like me to get you a strap to hang onto?" She said, "No, thanks, I have one." He said, "Then would you mind letting go of my necktie?"

In another jam-packed bus, the young lady was having difficulty fishing for a half dollar in her purse to pay her fare. A gentleman standing next to her volunteered, "May I pay your fare?" She stammered, "Oh no, I wouldn't let you do that. After all, you're a total stranger." He said, "Not really, you've unzippered me three times."

Mayor Koch wants to balance the budget by cutting services in New York City by $299 million and hiking taxes by $192 million . . . Well, for one thing, he won't need that many cops on 8th Avenue and Broadway because the Johns couldn't afford to shop for those broads, after taxes . . . The way Broadway and 8th Avenue is going, it won't be long before Sodom and Gomorrah will be considered model cities.

A member of the vice squad arrested a peddler on 42nd Street for selling pornographic photographs. "But these aren't dirty," the salesman complained. The officer pointed to one particularly intricate study of several naked men and women. The guy said, "Aw, c'mon man, ain't you ever seen five people in love before?"

I'm sure we won't miss the sanitationmen the mayor wants to cut. On my block the garbage has been there so long it's been declared a landmark.

The parking-garage tax would double. It will now cost more to park a car than run it . . . Koch also suggests raising taxes on unleaded and leaded gas. I always wanted to be a big spender—but not at a gas pump . . . Carpooling is a great gas saver and parking saver—just drive your car into a pool and leave it there.

Banks will be taxed another $20 million—the mayor is doing a better job on them than Willie Sutton.

Environmental protection drops 460 employees . . . The mayor says he'll save money by putting the street signs up in Braille . . . The people of Indiana say we have too much pollution, too much noise, too much crime. Okay, so in Terre Haute you won't get mugged—but you'll die of boredom.

The schools lose 7,186 employees . . . The kids won't miss the teachers. The hardest part of telling young people about the facts of life is finding something they don't already know.

The 17 municipal hospitals take a $20-million cut in their budget. It's really not the doctors or nurses or hospitals that are the problem, it's the side effects—like bankruptcy.

Everybody is always picking on our taxi drivers—and rightfully so. At school he couldn't find the shortest distance between two points—so he became a taxi driver. Rain is what makes flowers grow—and taxicabs disappear.

Even our crooks are more particular. I saw this guy in one department store the other day—he was comparison shoplifting.

Men who fail their driver's tests usually wind up as parking lot attendants.

Keeping a dog in the city keeps them healthy. Every morning I let my dog out and he runs for miles looking for a tree.

New York City is always having money problems. You can tell when a city is in financial trouble. Like when there's a three-alarm fire and the firemen have to take a bus.

I think my nephew may have a legitimate gripe when he complains about the teaching methods in his school. For example, the fire drill is a written test.

I know the number one salesman in the world. He sold a 50-gallon drum of black ink to my friend the mayor.

What a sight New York City must have been the night of the blackout. All the lights out, all the businesses closed, no one in the streets—sounds like any town in Connecticut after 8 P.M.

New York is the most crowded city of all, and no wonder. It's surrounded by all kinds of toll booths and toll roads—and they're all going up in price. Nobody can afford to leave.

I love New York. Where else can you find somebody to invest in a mutual fund with a welfare check?

The traffic situation has changed. Last year it took me an hour and a half to get from the airport to midtown. No more. That's all changed. Today it took two hours—and I was coming by helicopter.

It's about time we did something about crime today. You know juvenile delinquency has gotten out of hand when gun shops start running "Back To School Sales."

A friend of mine really lives in a rough neighborhood. Once a year he needs to hold a garage sale to get rid of all the stuff his kids stole!

One neighborhood in the Bronx is so rough—the most popular form of transportation is the stretcher.

I'll tell you how high the crime rate is in that neighborhood. If you live in a house that hasn't been robbed at least once in the past two weeks—you're dragged in for questioning.

People keep saying violence on TV isn't good for kids. Actually, it does have a practical use—it prepares kids for high school.

You don't think crime is everywhere? This guy I know was picked up on suspicion of robbery—and was mugged in the lineup.

Crime doesn't pay—or wouldn't if the government saw it. We don't seem to be able to check crime—so why don't we legalize it and tax it out of business?

Johnny Carson, who is always picking on New York, now admits that California has a bigger crime problem: "Yesterday I went downtown to wait in line to get some gas. I stuck my arm out for a right turn and someone took my watch."

My genius cousin took the wheels from a Cadillac, the grill from a Buick, the engine from a Rolls. And you know what he got?—Two years . . . Ken says: "The crime rate is really high. Last week while I was playing monopoly, someone was murdered in one of my hotels."

There are 22 mounted police in Central Park—but they refuse to get off the carousel . . . There is one neighborhood in the Bronx so tough, you could walk one block in any direction without leaving the scene of a crime.

You have to be smart to get along these days. One bright soul wore a mask all his life. He only took it off when he was robbing a bank . . . Another man pushed a gun at the paymaster and said, "Let the boys have their pay—just hand over the withholding taxes, hospitalization payments, group insurance premiums, and welfare funds."

Things had been extremely quiet around the police station for quite a while and the desk sergeant was worried. "I don't know what to think," he exclaimed one morning. "Here's a whole week gone by and no robberies, no murders, no drunk or disorderly cases—not even a traffic arrest. If something doesn't happen pretty soon they'll be laying us off!" "Don't worry about a thing, Sarge," replied a cop. "Something's bound to happen soon. I've still got a lot of faith in human nature!"

You think we have trouble. In Chicago they have so much violence that if they really like you—they give you the keys out of the city.

I don't trust my new neighbor. Before he gave me his business card—he shuffled them.

David Sayh grew up in the South Bronx, one of the highest crime-rate neighborhoods in the world. He says: "You call the police emergency number—they put you on hold and play music. They were looking for everybody in my neighborhood. We used to get arrest warrants in the mail addressed to 'Occupant.'"

Two guys were standing on a street corner in Brooklyn. One said to the other: "You wanna share a cab?" The other guy said, "Sure—you take the hubcaps—I'll take the battery."

I was going to read the report about the rising crime rate—but somebody stole it.

I'm not worried about crime in the streets—but in my neighborhood they make house calls.

Policemen just aren't the same any more. They used to be a regular part of the community; now the cop on my beat has an unlisted badge number.

The cop was competing in a rifle tournament. When his card was brought to him, it was such a poor performance that he involuntarily remarked to his captain who was scrutinizing it: "After looking at my card I feel like shooting myself." The captain said, "Better take two bullets."

Many prisons attempt to permit inmates to follow their regular trades while serving sentences. In one instance the warden asked a new man if he would like to pursue his normal trade in prison: "Sure would—I'm a traveling salesman."

Living in New York City is great, but it can be a bit of a nuisance. I have three locks on my door, besides a double bolt, a chain, and a burglar alarm—it takes me longer to get out than burglars to get in.

A friend in the Bronx told me: if Diogenes ever came through our neighborhood with his lamp—they'd steal it.

Sammy Kaye says he lives in a real rough neighborhood. Last year Santa Claus had his sled drawn by attack reindeer.

You know you're in a tough neighborhood when you go into a confessional and there's graffiti on the walls.

Mitch Krug says crime runs in the family: "The other night I was robbed by this little gray-haired lady. She said her son the mugger was home with the flu."

The P.T.A. people told the networks that if they don't cut out the violence on TV they are coming down and blow up the studio.

A man showed up at a Miami police station with an alligator and asked the sergeant at the desk what he should do. The officer suggested he take him to the zoo. The next day the sergeant was driving along Biscayne Boulevard and spotted the man with the alligator on a leash. "I thought I told you to take him to the zoo," the cop said. "I did," replied the guy, "and he had such a good time, that now we're going to Sea World."

I was in a hurry and told the taxi driver to take me to Greenwich Village. The driver asked, "Do you know how to go?" I said no. He said, "Leave everything to me." The meter read $132—we came through Connecticut. I said, "Why did we go this way?" He said, "I wanted to make the lights."

Most taxi drivers in New York have their "No Disturb" sign on when you're desperate for a cab—and the driver auditions you to make sure you are going where *he* wants to go.

And they've got all kinds of signs in their cabs: "No Smoking," "We cash nothing over $5," "Keep your feet off the seats," "No eating, drinking, or heavy breathing." One independent cabbie had this sign: "Please don't use the ashtrays while the maid is on vacation."

The cab was crawling in New York traffic and the lady passenger pleaded, "Please, mister, can't you go any faster?" "Sure, lady," said the cabbie. "But I ain't allowed to leave the taxi."

The cab driver was recklessly running in and out of traffic. The scared little lady in the back seat was frantic. "Please," she pleaded, "be a little more careful—I have twelve children at home."
    "Lady," the driver answered, "you're telling me to be careful?"

What most people would like to save for a rainy day is a taxi—the off-duty light on those New York cabs is wired to go on whenever it is touched by a drop of rain.

Gene Baylos was in a taxi that was hit by a passenger car. The door of the cab flew open and Gene found himself on the pavement in considerable pain. The cab driver, unhurt, cried, "Is there anything I can do?" Gene said, "Yeah, shut off your meter."

What's so bad about being a cab driver? Don't they go to work every morning in a taxi? And most of them are honest. I gave this cabbie a $10 bill instead of a $5 bill. He tried to catch me—he knocked on his window with a sponge.

The cabbie driving downhill says to his fare, "Lady, I think my brakes are gone." She said, "My God what are we gonna do?" He said, "Don't worry—there's a stop sign at the bottom of the hill."

Of course it isn't easy for cab drivers with the New York traffic . . . Nobody pays attention to speed limits these days. The only people you see doing 55 miles per hour are kids on skateboards . . . And did you ever get in one of those traffic jams on the Long Island Expressway? I was in one that was so bad—it's the first time I was ever passed by an abandoned car.

The cop stopped the cab driver. "You idiot," he yelled, "how could you hit a man in broad daylight going 20 miles an hour?" The cabbie said, "I'm sorry—my windshield is covered with safety stickers—I couldn't see a thing . . ." You can't always blame the cabbie. One taxi driver was waiting for a traffic light to change when he was bumped from behind. He calmly stepped out of his cab and walked back to the lady who hit him. "Tell me something," he snarled, "I'm curious—how do you stop when I'm not here?"

If crime doesn't pay, how come it's one of the biggest businesses in the U.S.? . . . I know one guy whose ambition in life is to become a good hostage . . . I know another who had his name changed to Hilton to match his towels . . . Making money isn't the real problem in his life—the trouble is passing it.

I came from a pretty tough neighborhood. Nothing but killings. I went out and bought a water bed—there was a guy at the bottom of it.

I live in a very interesting neighborhood. I live in the only neighborhood where I plan a budget and I allow for holdup money.

"Does your family know you're a thief?" I asked this character. He said, "My mother found out. One night she came to my house for dinner and we were using her silverware."

Crime is up 26%—and that's not counting the new gas prices . . . Crime doesn't pay—but at least you don't have to declare it on your income tax . . . Everybody has a suggestion for crime prevention. Mayor Koch says the girls should not wear gold chains or anything that glitters. One woman suggested she had the answer to all this crime in the streets: "He who steals my purse—steals 15 credit cards."

In one neighborhood in the Bronx there is so much crime, the local church has an unlisted number . . . It's such a rough neighborhood, the Avon lady goes door to door selling bullet proof makeup . . . I dreamed I was mugged by an out-of-work bus driver—but he wouldn't take my money because I didn't have the exact change.

The bandit held up a gas station and took every cent in the place and roared away in a car—then roared back three minutes later. "You got all our money, what do you want now?" the owner asked, "I just remembered your sign said you give trading stamps."

There's one thing you can say for the Mafia: They're one of the few groups who still make house calls . . . The neighborhood gal was berating her hood boyfriend for forgetting her birthday. "Gee," he apologized. "I didn't forget it. I wanted to get you something special. I even went to the jewelry shop to get you something but he was still open."

There was an embarrassing scene on Capitol Hill in Washington. A cop was chasing a purse snatcher and when he yelled, "Stop thief," three Congressmen froze.

An apartment in Brooklyn had a neatly lettered sign on the door which read: "This apartment has been robbed four times. I have also been mugged on the street twice. No diamonds—no cash—no booze. Fur coats are 15 years old. My radio and TV have already been ripped off. Camera has cracked lens." That's right—somebody stole the sign.